Creating Celebration Quilts

Your Guide to Making Memory Quilts

Cyndi Souder

Foreword by Pat Sloan

Schiffer Publishing Ltd

4880 Lower Valley Road • Atglen, PA 19310

Published by Schiffer Publishing, Ltd.
4880 Lower Valley Road
Atglen, PA 19310
Phone: (610) 593-1777; Fax: (610) 593-2002
E-mail: Info@schifferbooks.com

For the largest selection of fine reference books on this and related
subjects, please visit our website at:
www.schifferbooks.com.
You may also write for a free catalog.
This book may be purchased from the publisher.
Please try your bookstore first.
We are always looking for people to write books on new and related
subjects. If you have an idea for a book, please contact us at:
proposals@schifferbooks.com.

Schiffer Books are available at special discounts for bulk purchases for
sales promotions or premiums. Special editions, including personalized
covers, corporate imprints, and excerpts can be created in large quanti-
ties for special needs. For more information contact the publisher.

In Europe, Schiffer books are distributed by
Bushwood Books
6 Marksbury Ave.
Kew Gardens
Surrey TW9 4JF England
Phone: 44 (0) 20 8392 8585; Fax: 44 (0) 20 8392 9876
E-mail: info@bushwoodbooks.co.uk
Website: www.bushwoodbooks.co.uk

Dedication

To my husband Eric, who has made this journey possible.

Copyright © 2013 by Cyndi Souder
Library of Congress Control Number: 2013930173

Designed by RoS
Type set in AvantGarde/Fontana

ISBN: 978-0-7643-4350-6
Printed in China

Other Schiffer Books on Related Subjects:
A Quilted Memory: Ideas and Inspiration for Reusing Vintage Textiles,
978-0-7643-3921-9, $19.99
Creating Children's Artwork Quilts,
978-0-7643-4180-9, $16.99
Quilts in Everyday Life, 1855-1955: A 100-Year Photographic History,
978-0-7643-4216-5, $34.99

Contents

Foreword

When Cyndi told me she was writing a book about creating Celebration Quilts, I knew a winner was being born. Cyndi's love for and devotion to creating a quilt with memories is strong. She not only has made them to celebrate people close to her, like "Teal Beauty," which was made in memory of her sister, but she has also been on a quest to help others create these quilts with meaning. Not just meaning, though... Cyndi helps you bring depth and excitement to those memories.

Quilts with memories, quilts that celebrate, quilts to record...They have been around for a very long time. Cyndi brings a fresh look at using your clothing, scraps, and tidbits in a quilt that will capture the essence of the person, the place, or the moment.

From taking that first little thought of a quilt, to creating the concept and gathering the supplies, Cyndi has broken the process down for you. She helps you make excellent decisions so you select what works best for memories. Many of these quilts are "one of a kind" creations that evolve as you work, but many quilters love using patterns so that they can enjoy working without the worry of designing. Three quilts in this book are based on existing patterns, traditional blocks, or packaged precut strips, ensuring that quilters have everything they will need.

One of the main reasons I quilt is the stories. The stories I hear about quilts when I travel to teach fill my soul. It's the reason I go see antique quilts in museums: to read the stories or wonder what they are. The stories are the reasons I continue to find quilting exciting after twenty years.

If you have a desire to make a quilt that tells a story, either in memory of someone special or just because you want to, I know you are going to enjoy this book.

Let the memories live on in your quilts. I can't wait to see them!

Pat Sloan
www.PatSloan.com

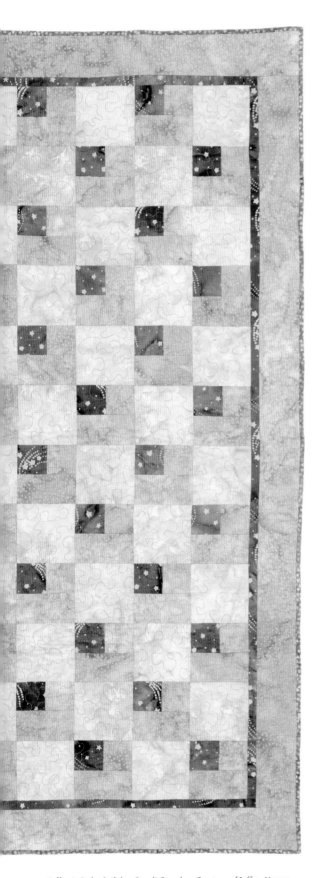

Preface

I've been quilting since 1980, and I have been making Celebration Quilts since the 1990s. I have made quilts to celebrate births, birthdays, adoptions, weddings, anniversaries, life events, world events, and the lives of lost loved ones. These are all Celebration Quilts.

When I teach my Celebration Quilts workshop, I meet all kinds of quilters — beginners and experienced quilters, traditional and art quilters, quilters who work alone and quilters who work in groups. The thing they all have in common is their desire to create. In the workshop, many of my students want to pay tribute to family members who have passed on. Some students want to honor something from their own lives, like a career or an overseas deployment. Others want to find a way to use items from their past in their current work.

Regardless of your quilting experience or skill level, you can make Celebration Quilts that are meaningful. My goal is to give you the tools to plan and create your own Celebration Quilts.

In this book, you'll find lots of examples of Celebration Quilts. You'll see how I used my Celebration Quilt Worksheet to help with the design process for five special Celebration Quilts. You'll add to your own skills toolbox when you read about taming difficult fabrics, using photographs in quilts, making hanging sleeves, and labeling your quilts. Finally, I hope you will be inspired by these stories and this collection of quilts.

Jeffrey's Baby Quilt by Cyndi Souder. *Courtesy of Jeffrey Young.*

To Mary, Who Has Kept Us All Rolling Along
by Cyndi Souder.

Acknowledgments

Thank you to my first teachers, who are no longer sewing with us: To Nana, who taught me to hand sew; to Vicki, who taught me to sew garments by machine and quilts by hand; and to Mom, for whom no sewing project was too complicated.

Thank you, Eric, for your patience, your support, and your great ideas. Go, TS!

Thank you to my readers: Lisa Ellis, Kathy Lincoln, Helen Mitternight, and Karen Young; you made this a better book.

Thank you to my MMS support team: Kathy Lincoln and Mary Kerr; your motivation, patience, and encouragement kept me going throughout this process. You guys rock!

Thank you to my quilt clients for trusting me with your thoughts, visions, and precious artifacts. I want to specifically thank Wendy Luke and Linda Lee Kaye for allowing me to so publicly relive the process through which we created your Celebration Quilts. Thank you, Nancy and Neil Weidner, for graciously returning *Teal Beauty* to me for photography and for your support of the Institute for Cancer Research.

Thank you, Teal Beauty Quilters! The quilt, the story, and your generosity live on! Teal Beauty Quilters include Beverly Burroughs, Karen Burshnick, Linda Cooper, Karen Dever, Annabel Ebersole, Lisa Ellis, Carol Fray, Libby Fritsche, Kathye Gillette, Cathie Hoover, Susie Johnson, Mary Kerr, Kathy Lincoln, Jeannie Minchak, Jeannette Muir, Bonnie Prouty, Claudia Sammis, Linda Snow, Diane Yim, and me! Also, thank you, Bruce Magidson of SewBatik.com, for your support of the Teal Beauty project.

Thank you to my students and quilting friends who so generously shared their work for the sake of the book. Thank you to my family and friends who have returned my quilts for photography. It was so wonderful to see my quilts coming home to visit for a while! Thank you, Pat Sloan, for your confidence, generosity, and enthusiasm. And thank you to everyone who has patiently endured my focused obsession with this project throughout the process.

Introduction
About Celebration Quilts

In the simplest terms, Celebration Quilts are quilts designed to celebrate something. They may welcome a new life into the world or welcome a new family member by celebrating a wedding or an adoption. They may pay tribute to a lost loved one, someone recently departed or from generations ago. Celebration Quilts commemorate occasions or events, sometimes happy and sometimes serious. They freeze a moment in time and hold it there in fabric for you to revisit later.

Throughout the book, I use the term "artifacts" to refer to the items, objects, and treasures through which we access memories and emotions. Artifacts can be clothing, linens, personal effects, books, or photographs — anything that can transport us to another time or place. Artifacts are pathways to memories and can be used to evoke those same memories in your Celebration Quilts.

When I made *Memories* (page 11), I based the quilt on a photograph my father took of my sister sunbathing in our backyard. In the photo, she was wearing her favorite sunglasses. I later acquired those old sunglasses and added them to the quilt. Whenever I see those sunglasses hanging from the quilt, I am transported to my old backyard, sitting in the sun with my sister.

Teal Beauty (page 20) resulted from my desire to honor my sister's life and raise funds for cancer research. I chose an existing commercial pattern, a color palette, and a group of friends to help. I made *Flying Pumpkins* (page 36) as a holiday gift for my brother-in-law. I wanted to give him a quilt that he could use and that would honor his ongoing involvement with the World Championship Punkin Chunkin. *Flying Pumpkins* is based on a traditional nine-patch block.

The term "Celebration Quilt" covers a lot of ground. When quilts celebrate a person's life, I often call these Tribute Quilts. Quilts that incorporate tee shirts or other artifacts are sometimes called Memory Quilts. These quilts all fall under the umbrella of Celebration Quilts.

Remembering Pride and Joy I and II by Shannon Shirley. Notice the special shirt pockets integrated into the quilt (see closeup). *Courtesy of the artist.*

Quilts Based on Existing Patterns or Traditional Blocks

Celebration Quilts can be made from traditional quilt blocks or purchased patterns. What makes these quilts special can be the fabrics, the colors, or the block itself. Baby quilts are often made from patterns or traditional blocks.

Quilts that Start with an Idea

Occasionally, an event will inspire us to create a Celebration Quilt. These quilts begin with a concept: the decorating scheme for a baby's room, a milestone birthday, a life-changing news event, or an experience that you want to capture and remember forever. For these Celebration Quilts, the quilt design emerges from the idea and the materials are chosen to support the concept. *Mentor, Guru and Sage* (page 30) started with a concept and a collection of bowties. The *Strippy Baby Quilt* (page 26) was the perfect marriage between my desire to create a happy gender-neutral baby quilt and a beautiful pack of precut batik strips.

Quilts Designed Around Artifacts

Sometimes, Celebration Quilts begin with physical things: a drawer full of tee shirts, a closet of clothing left behind, a box of linens found in an attic, or long-forgotten pictures that are unexpectedly recovered. In these cases, the Celebration Quilt is designed around the items you want to include. The artifacts drive the design process. *Too Much Soul to Control* (page 41) is a good example of this approach.

How to Use this Book

This book is not meant to be read in order. Choose the section you want and start there. Specifically, the book includes:

1. The Celebration Quilts Worksheet

Located on page 10, this will help you each time you begin a new Celebration Quilt. You can use it to choose a pattern or develop a design, choose colors and fabrics, and decide on any artifacts you may want to have in your quilt.

2. A Closer Look

This section includes more in depth information on the five quilts featured in this book. Here you will get the story behind the quilt, the completed Celebration Quilt Worksheet for each quilt, and more information about the design and construction process.

3. Celebration Quilts Toolbox

This contains useful information about the nuts and bolts of making Celebration Quilts, including:

- **TAMING DIFFICULT FABRICS** has tips for working with knits (including tee shirts), silk, and sheer fabrics.

- **USING PHOTOGRAPHS** will help you figure out how to incorporate images into your quilts.

- **QUILTING TIPS** outlines what to quilt first and gives hints for adding quilted words to your quilts.

- **HANGING SLEEVES** gives you step-by-step instructions for making a hanging sleeve for wall quilts and for quilts that may hang in shows.

- **ALL ABOUT LABELS** provides guidelines and tips for creating useful and creative documentation for your quilts.

4. Gallery of Celebration Quilts

Are you looking for some inspiration? If so, then check out this gallery of completed works beginning on page 68 for ideas. There are examples of quilts for many different occasions and purposes.

The Celebration Quilt Worksheet

Creating Celebration Quilts often requires special thought and decisions, which is why I created this worksheet. It will help guide you through the design process. You may not need to spend much time on all of the ten questions, but addressing each of the questions, however briefly, will help ensure that you are headed in a design direction that makes sense for your quilt.

I recommend photocopying the worksheet and then filling it out by hand. Use an extra sheet of paper for answers that won't fit on the lines or for sketching. To help you fully answer the questions, see the in depth explanations for each of them on the pages following the worksheet.

You Have My Permission!

This is very important, so read carefully. Make only those quilts that you want to make. Seriously. I give you permission.

You do not have to make quilts for distant relatives who might be better served by a commercial quilt that they can use under a beach picnic. You do not have to make baby quilts for everyone in your office who has a baby unless you genuinely want to make quilts for them. And you do not have to make really complicated patterns in colors you hate just because someone is getting married.

If you feel you must make a quilt to honor an occasion, find the middle ground between what you want to make and what they would like to receive. It's better to make a quilt that you both really like than it is to make a quilt they love and you resent. Think about it.

The Celebration Quilt Worksheet

The Purpose of the Quilt

1. What or whom will this quilt commemorate?
_____
_____
_____

2. Describe the person, life, or event you are commemorating.
_____
_____
_____

The Mechanics of the Quilt

3. Describe the quilt's environment.
_____
_____
_____

4. How will the quilt be used?
_____
_____
_____

5. How big will this quilt be?
_____
_____
_____

The Design of the Quilt

6. What effect do you want to achieve with this quilt?
_____
_____
_____

7. Do you have specific colors, shapes, patterns in mind?
_____
_____
_____

8. What artifacts do you have that you want to include?
_____
_____
_____

9. What will you need to add to complete this quilt?
_____
_____
_____

10. Describe the quilt. Include colors, materials, anything and everything you are considering. Feel free to sketch.
_____
_____

The Purpose of the Quilt

1. What or whom will this quilt commemorate?

This question seems easy to answer, but it's the one question that really stymies some of the students who have been through my workshop. The most common mistake is to try to do too much in one quilt. The key here is to focus.

What are you celebrating? Is your topic a person? An event? An accomplishment? For example:
• Are you using tee shirts to celebrate athletic achievement?
• Are you saving baby clothes to celebrate the next generation of your family?
• Do you have a collection of a lost loved one's clothing that you cannot discard?

I have a list of quilts in my head that I would like to make to celebrate my sister's life. We were very close and I miss her every day. I could try to create just one quilt about my sister, but what would I commemorate? Her skills as a seamstress? The fact that she taught me to quilt? Her prize orchids? Her love of all things French? The ovarian cancer that took her life? There's just too much for all of that to be in one quilt! Any one of those topics would be enough. To make a successful Celebration Quilt, I need to break it down. I need to focus on one aspect of her life that I can portray effectively in a quilt. In fact, I have celebrated her life through three quilts so far:

Memories by Cyndi Souder.

• *Memories* celebrates her teenage years when she was still living in our childhood home. The quilt is based on one of my father's photographs.

• *A Circle of Friends* celebrates the years of quilting immediately before her death and my amazing quilter friends who embraced her and pulled her into our circle.

• *Teal Beauty* (page 20) celebrates her valiant battle against ovarian cancer and my niece's commitment to raising funds for cancer research.

Try to identify the exact thing you're celebrating. Narrow your focus as much as possible. It will make the design process easier and the quilt will have more impact.

2. Describe the person, life, or event you are commemorating.

Once you've identified the focus of your quilt, it's time to describe that focus. Write down everything that you can think of relating to the focus of your quilt.

If you're celebrating a person, describe that person in as much detail as you can. When I made *Too Much Soul to Control* (page 41), I sat with my client on several occasions to learn more about her late husband before I designed the quilt. He loved to cook and he loved to eat. He loved to travel and he especially loved clothes. He was larger than life, energetic, charismatic, and good-natured. People wanted to know him. He was the life of the party.

A Circle of Friends by Cyndi Souder. Notice the QuiltWriting on the left and right borders.

Too Much Soul to Control by Cyndi Souder.
Courtesy of Linda Lee Kaye.

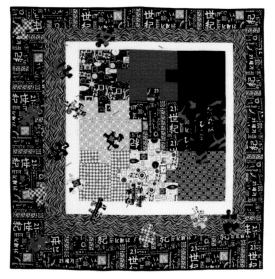

A Puzzling Year by Cyndi Souder
commemorated the year 2000.

Rather than concentrate on what she had lost, my client wanted to celebrate the energy of her husband's life. He had too much soul to control. When you look at the quilt, do you see the energy?

Don't edit the descriptions; just write. You probably won't use all of the information, but it's better to have too much inspiration than not enough. When in doubt, write it down.

If your focus is a person, then consider these six things: lifestyle, personality traits, favorite activities, favorite colors, favorite places to live or travel, and favorite foods or drinks.

If your focus is an event, then consider these four questions: What's the event (birth, graduation, marriage, special achievement, death)? What are the circumstances surrounding the event? Where and when did the event take place? If you want to transport the viewer back to the event — like a wedding — is there a special detail you could include?

The Mechanics of the Quilt

If you know where the quilt will live and how it will be treated, then some of your design decisions will become simple.

3. Describe the quilt's environment.
Will this quilt live under your care or will someone else care for it? Even if you are keeping the quilt, you should consider these questions:

• WILL THIS QUILT BE KEPT IN DIRECT SUNLIGHT? If so, then fading may be an issue. There are products on the market that advertise they will keep your fabrics from fading, but I have not tried them. If the original plan is to keep the quilt in direct sunlight, I strongly recommend that you reconsider.

• WILL ANIMALS HAVE ACCESS TO THIS QUILT? Will the quilt be folded over the back of the sofa where the cat hangs out or on the foot of the bed where the puppies sleep? If so, consider using durable fabric that can be laundered often. Quilts that are shared with pets generally have a shorter life span. If you want the quilt are you are planning to survive a long time, consider making the quilt to hang on a wall.

• WILL CHILDREN HAVE ACCESS TO THIS QUILT? If so, be careful with embellishments. You don't want to create a choking hazard by adding beads or buttons to the surface of a quilt. You may also want to construct your quilt to withstand the laundry.

• IT'S LIKELY THAT OUR QUILTS WILL OUTLIVE US. WHERE WILL YOUR QUILT GO NEXT? Who would appreciate having your quilt? Did someone help you make it? Consider making this decision official and include it in your will. If you are planning to leave it to an institution or museum, it's a good idea to make these arrangements in advance to ensure the institution wants your quilt and has the resources to care for it properly. Without making other plans, your quilt could become part of someone's garage sale or used as padding in a moving van. Don't let that happen!

4. How will the Quilt be used?

Will this quilt be displayed? Will it be hung on a wall as art or used for physical warmth and comfort? Once you know this, then you can make construction, surface design, and embellishment decisions.

Early in my quilting career, traditional quilts went on beds and art quilts went on the wall. Now, traditional quilts are considered art and the line between traditional and art is blurring.

I divide quilts into two categories: Utility Quilts and Wall Quilts. Utility quilts are used and sometimes abused. They are put on beds, on sofas, on the floor, and on the grass for picnics. They are often machine washed and will show signs of wear. Wall quilts hang on the wall. They will never see the inside of a washing machine and are not designed to keep anyone physically warm.

Utility Quilts

Here are some things to consider if you're making a Celebration Quilt that will be used:

- **CLEANING AND DURABILITY.** If people will use this quilt (put it on the bed, take it to college, wrap up in it to watch TV), then give some thought to cleaning and durability. This also applies to table runners and quilted pillows. Consider using materials that will last and survive potential wear. Cotton is generally a good choice. Silk and velvet are lovely to touch, but they may not weather the washing machine very well.

- **TEXTURE.** Think about how the quilt will feel to your hand. Some fabrics feel rough and would be inappropriate for a quilt meant to comfort someone who is sick. When I make chemo quilts for cancer patients, I try to use flannel. It's durable and it feels nice. Microfiber and fleece are other good choices if soft texture is your goal.

- **SPECIAL CONSIDERATIONS FOR CHILDREN'S QUILTS.** If this quilt is meant for a child, consider the age of the lucky recipient. If the quilt is for an infant, then avoid beading or any surface design technique (painting, for example) that could be toxic to the child. While it's fun to make a pocket with a button flap for a toddler, an infant could choke on that button. Think Velcro® instead. For toddlers, consider including activities like pockets or games. For a military family, consider including a picture of the family member who may be deployed. For more information on using photographs, see page 52.

Wall Quilts

For Celebration Quilts that will be hung on a wall and not used, here are some things to consider:

- **HOW WILL THIS QUILT BE HUNG?** For my wall quilts, I add a sleeve at the top so that the owner can insert a wooden slat or a hanging rod to support the quilt. If your quilt will be exhibited at a quilt show, then make sure the sleeve is large enough to accommodate the larger poles in the standard pipe-and-drape setup many quilt shows use. See page 61 for more information about making a sleeve for your quilt.

Adam's Baby Quilt by Cyndi Souder. *Courtesy of Adam Greve.* The gold is Minkee, providing a wonderful texture.

- **WILL THIS QUILT HAVE A LOT OF PHYSICALLY HEAVY EMBELLISHMENT ON IT?** For one client's project, I planned to use beads, pearls, beach glass, and anything else I could attach to the quilt that would support my design ideas. I knew this had the potential to distort the quilt when it hung on the wall. To address this, I added a layer of buckram, an interfacing often used for stability and shaping. When I added the beads, I made sure to catch the buckram in most of my stitches so that the layers would stay together and the center of the quilt would not bow away from the wall under the weight. If an extra layer of stabilization won't work, consider stretcher bars or some other internal structure. If your quilt is especially large or heavy, you may need to reinforce your hanging system. Consider special anchors or supports that can accommodate the additional weight.

- **WILL THIS QUILT HANG STRAIGHT AND FLAT UNDER THE STRAIN OF YOUR EMBELLISHMENTS?** This was my concern for one particularly heavy commission quilt. In addition, the quilt would be seen first from the side, which would highlight any areas that bow out or hang awkwardly. To combat this, I borrowed a trick from Coco Chanel. To ensure that her jackets hung straight, she added weight in the hem. For this quilt, I added a sleeve across the bottom and inserted a thin metal slat. The weight keeps the quilt hanging straight.

- **HOW WILL THE OWNER CARE FOR THE QUILT?** With the normal passage of time, quilts get dusty. Give some thought to care instructions and be sure to share them. Consider creating a separate label for this purpose. Options include machine wash and dry, dry clean only, brush lightly, dust with a lint roller, or vacuum through a screen. The method you recommend depends on the materials and the construction of the quilt.

- **WILL THE QUILT BE FRAMED?** When I participated in the group project "Healing Quilts in Medicine," the Walter Reed Army Medical Center required us to frame our quilts in Plexiglas® box frames. If you are framing your quilt, consider how thick the quilt is — including any embellishments you're going to add. If you are planning three-dimensional appliqué or thick beading, that can add considerably to the overall thickness of the quilt. Make sure the frame will accommodate any additional depth.

5. How big will this quilt be?

Sometimes the subject matter dictates the size of the finished quilt. More often, however, the quilt is made to fit a certain space or a specific piece of furniture. Before you start work, consider these points:

- **IS THIS QUILT DESTINED FOR A BED?** If so, will it function as a bedspread or just an extra layer for looks and warmth? If this quilt will be the main bed covering, make sure you know the size of the bed and add enough "drop" on each side. With the variety of mattress sizes available, it's a good idea to measure the bed before you plan the quilt. To paraphrase a wise soul, "Measure twice, sew once."

- **WILL THIS QUILT HANG ON A WALL?** If so, make sure it will fit in the space you have in mind. My clients often have a specific place in mind when they commission a quilt, and the finished quilt must hang well in that space. For one project, we taped newspaper in different shapes and sizes on the wall until we could identify the right dimensions for the space.

- **ARE YOU PLANNING TO USE A STIFF STABILIZER (LIKE TIMTEX® OR PELTEX®) IN THE QUILT?** If so, this may limit the overall size of your quilt to what you can reasonably fit on your machine. If you roll some stiff stabilizers, they lose their fresh, flat appearance and may never lay completely flat again.

- **DO YOU PLAN TO DO THE QUILTING YOURSELF OR WILL YOU QUILT BY CHECK (HIRE SOMEONE ELSE TO DO THE QUILTING)?** If you're quilting this project yourself, make sure you are comfortable with the overall size. You may prefer working on a wall quilt or a twin size rather than a California king.

Sometimes we need help completing our quilts. Whether you want hand or machine quilting, I am in favor of using the services of quilters for hire. Many of my bed-size quilts display the work of professional longarm quilters. Before handing your quilt top over to someone else, though, make sure you are comfortable with their work, pricing, and schedule. Ask lots of questions. I like speaking with other people who have hired the quilter and seeing some of the quilter's work. In a perfect world, I like to give an audition quilt (often a class sample) to the quilter to establish a working relationship. Communication is key. Be clear about your hopes and expectations.

6. What effect do you want to achieve with this quilt?

I love it when a quilt catches my eye and I know right away what it's about. Some quilts just broadcast a vibe from across a room. What do you want your quilt to say?

• **Is the subject of your quilt happy and upbeat?** Are you celebrating a happy occasion? If so, choose colors and materials to reflect that. Light and bright may be the way to do that. Keep this in mind when you move beyond colors and into design. Active designs like circles may reinforce your happy theme.

• **Do you want your quilt to convey serious or somber feelings?** Then consider choosing colors and materials that support that. Black is predictable, but I still use it in almost every quilt. You may want to consider using darker colors that may be unexpected, like eggplant, burnt orange, or midnight blue. For your design, you may want to stick with more static patterns with less movement. Straight lines and square shapes may help support the serious mood.

• **Are you celebrating someone who is or was orderly and tidy?** Think about using grids or repeated regular shapes in your quilt design.

• **Is the subject of your quilt more carefree and wild?** Think about working with abstract and loosey-goosey (Yes, that's a technical term!) designs to convey the feeling you want to express.

7. Do you have specific colors, shapes, patterns in mind?

By this point in the design process, you probably have some ideas in mind. Before you move forward with them, though, ask yourself these questions:

• **Have you chosen these colors because you like them or because they would work best for this quilt?** It may not matter, especially if you're making the quilt for yourself. However, if you are making a quilt to celebrate a person or an event, consider using colors that reflect your subject. For example, I love using black and taupe together, but I probably wouldn't use them for a baby quilt. It would all depend on the baby's parents.

• **Do you have shapes or patterns in mind for this quilt?** Ask yourself why you made these particular choices. Do *you* like them or are they good choices for your subject matter?

• **Do you like where this design is going?** If this quilt is for someone else, you must balance what you want to make with what they will want to receive. If you hate the quilt design, either change the design or gracefully decline. Do not make the quilt if you won't like working on it. You have my permission.

• **Will the colors and other design elements harmonize with where the quilt will go?** Does it matter? I remember seeing a bumper sticker that said "Art doesn't have to match the sofa." Make sure you know if it matters for your quilt.

• **Will you use an existing pattern or your own original design?** Try not to get stuck on creating an original design for special quilts. It's perfectly fine to

Faith and Love by Cyndi Souder. *Courtesy of Suzanne Souder and Glenn Rill.* The center panel is a rubbing on muslin made from a gravestone at a cemetery of a local church.

Family by Judy Vincentz Gula. *Courtesy of Pat and Chet Vincentz.*

The Write Stuff by Cyndi Souder. The antique pen near the bottom of the quilt is from my grandmother's writing desk.

use a traditional design or an existing pattern unless you're working for a client who is expecting original work. You could also consider starting with a traditional design and making it your own by using unconventional colors or changing the scale of the pieces or using it as a background for an interesting appliqué or surface design. *Voyages* by Kathy Lincoln (page 72) combines the traditional storm at sea pattern with printing photographs on fabric.

8. What artifacts do you have that you want to include?

Celebration Quilts often start with an artifact. This could be a small linen collection, clothing, pictures, an invitation, or something you cannot bear to throw away. Maybe the artifact reminds you of a person or event that you feel strongly about and want to honor in some way.

Choosing Your Materials

Now you finally get to play with the stuff you want to include in the quilt, but what can you use and what should you leave for another project?

- **LOOK AT WHAT YOU HAVE.** Lay out all of the artifacts so that you can see them. Leave editing for later. Don't rule anything out until you can see it all at one time. I like to empty all horizontal surfaces in my studio and spread everything out — all of the clothing, pictures, and artifacts with which I plan to work.

- **LOOK FOR SIMILARITIES.** In making a Celebration Quilt, my primary challenge is to balance the concept with how the quilt will look. I want the quilt to be meaningful, but I also want it to have good design and good composition.

I start by looking for things that go together. Is there a color that stands out? Or a collection of colors that play well together? Color is a great unifying force. Do you have a collection of similar things that are different sizes? If they are alike enough in structure but different in scale, then that could provide you with repetition and variety. (Think children's clothes with matching doll outfits.)

Sort your artifacts into groups that work together or pull the things that clearly don't belong and leave the rest. Look for a color, shape, material, concept, any common thread that connects the items in the group. My greatest challenge in making *Too Much Soul to Control* (page 41) was finding that common thread. The subject of the quilt was so well-rounded and had so many varied interests! At first, I thought this project would have to be multiple quilts or most of the artifacts would have to be left for another time. When my client mentioned how important films were to her and her husband, I had my common thread and the design came together.

Other Things to Consider

- **DO YOU HAVE SO MANY THINGS THAT YOU HAVE MULTIPLE QUILTS?** This is the issue I encounter most often in my workshops. If you have twenty aprons and you want to make a wall quilt, that's a design challenge. You may want to pick a few favorites and use them. If it works out, then use some of the remaining artifacts to work in a series or to make gift quilts for others who would appreciate the history and meaning of your quilts.

After I completed *Mentor, Guru and Sage* (page 30), my client asked if there were more bow tie scraps. There were three adult children involved and she wanted me to make three quiltlets (small quilts) so that each child could have a wall quilt by which they could remember their father.

• **WILL YOU INCLUDE THE ACTUAL ARTIFACT OR A REPRESENTATION OF THE ARTIFACT?** Sometimes the artifacts you have are too big (a stuffed animal), too heavy (framed artwork), or too valuable (diamond jewelry) to include on a quilt. In this case, phototransfer might be the answer. Or, you could create the image using any of the appliqué or piecing techniques that you have in your quilting toolbox. When I created *Power Suited Him*, I wanted to use materials from the Power Suits Art Quilt Challenge to create a portrait of my father. I could have used a phototransfer, but the method I used seemed to suit my father's artistic nature.

• **WILL THE ARTIFACTS DAMAGE THE QUILT? CAN YOU MAKE THEM SAFE?** Will the artifact tarnish, degrade over time, or leave a residue? In this case, I'm thinking about silver charms, some plastics, and anything with adhesive. If there's any chance you're attaching something that could damage your quilt, think of how you can create an extra layer between the quilt and the artifact – or consider leaving the artifact elsewhere and simply refer to it. Could you use words or pictures?

• **HOW WILL YOU ATTACH THE ARTIFACTS?** If there are holes, you can sew the item to the quilt. If the item is small, you can still sew it down by stitching across the surface. In *Too Much Soul to Control* (page 41), I attached a cooking school medal, a watch, and a pair of reading glasses, all with thread.

• **IF THE ARTIFACT IS TOO BIG, WHAT ARE YOUR OPTIONS?** How big is too big? If your quilt will look like the artifact has a quilt stuck on it rather than a quilt featuring an artifact, then the item is too big. (Think "The tail is wagging the dog.") If it makes the quilt too heavy or too thick, it's too big. If you're thinking about whether it's too big, then that could be your clue.

If the artifact is too big, then think about ways to represent or refer to the artifact without actually including it. For example, what if you are trying to include a large stuffed bear made by a beloved aunt? If the bear's not flat, then it probably won't work. What if you included a picture of the bear, documented the story, and then unstuffed the bear and used the pelt flat or cut up the fur to include as a material? This could work especially well if the bear is too well-loved and won't stand up to much more handling.

9. What will you need to add to complete this quilt?

Sometimes you're lucky enough to have everything you need – all of the fabric for backgrounds, bindings, backings, labels, and sleeves. Generally, I've always had to add some things that were not in the collection we discussed in Question 8.

In *Too Much Soul to Control* (page 41), I added black fabric for the film frames and binding. Everything else, including the red tee shirt fabric used as the background, came from my client.

Power Suited Him by Cyndi Souder. I used this portrait of my father in the Power Suits Art Quilt Challenge.

Seashells by the Seashore by Judy Vincentz Gula. *Courtesy of the artist.*

In *Mentor, Guru and Sage* (page 30), I added black and burgundy silks. All other fabrics are from the collection of bow ties.

What else will you need to complete this quilt? Here are some things to consider:

- **WHAT WILL YOU USE FOR ANY BACKGROUNDS?** Sometimes all you need to bring together the artifacts and fabrics you have collected is one consistent background fabric. Or perhaps you could piece a background out of some of your fabrics and affix the artifacts to this pieced background. For example, what if you had a collection of baby spoons and baby clothes? You could use the clothing to piece a background and affix the small, lightweight spoons using thread or ribbons.

- **WHAT WILL YOU USE FOR BINDING? WILL YOU BIND THE QUILT?** Traditionally, quilts are bound. This gives the eye a place to stop and a signal to turn around and go back to the center of the quilt where the action is. I like to bind my quilts in a darker color value, often black, to further enclose the composition. If you think binding your quilt will be a distraction, there are other edge finishes for you to consider.

- **LABEL!** No quilt is complete without a label. This is the perfect place to include photos, dates, genealogy, your name, and any other factoids that could be relevant. Tell the story. The label will need to stand in for you when you cannot be there to explain the quilt in person. Read more about labels on page 63.

10. Describe the quilt. Include colors, materials, anything, and everything you are considering. Feel free to sketch.

I usually start the design process with the materials and hope they suggest a design direction. If they do, then I explore that and see how it works with the overall feeling that I'm trying to accomplish. If the materials do not lead me in any fruitful direction, then I start thinking about the concept. If ideas don't come right away, then take a break or page through the Gallery of Celebration Quilts starting on page 68. When you come back, play with the materials and artifacts you have. Sort them, fold them, clean or polish them. Ideas will come. Be patient.

Section One:

A Closer Look

When I lost my sister to ovarian cancer, I foundered. I made a few memorial quilts to celebrate her life, but they seemed small and inconsequential. My sister made a huge difference, not only in my life, but also in the lives of many others around her. In that tradition, I wanted to do something that was bigger than I was — something that could make a difference in someone else's life. The result was Teal Beauty.

Worksheet for Teal Beauty

1. **WHAT OR WHOM WILL THIS QUILT COMMEMORATE?** *Teal Beauty* was created to commemorate my sister, Victoria Zacheis Greve. She succumbed to ovarian cancer in 2004 after a courageous 4½-year battle. She was fifty-eight years old.

2. **DESCRIBE THE PERSON, LIFE, OR EVENT YOU ARE COMMEMORATING.** My sister had a love affair with all things fiber. She loved to sew garments for herself, her children, and me. She especially enjoyed handwork, filling most spare moments with needlepoint. When she learned to quilt, she taught me. Vicki was smart, organized, project-oriented, philanthropic, and fiercely loyal. She was generous with her time and her resources, always believing the best of people. I benefitted more than I can say from her generosity and encouragement.

3. **DESCRIBE THE QUILT'S ENVIRONMENT.** Once I knew that I wanted to do something big, I realized this quilt would be a fundraiser. Because I didn't know who would buy it, I didn't know where it would ultimately live. Because of this, I chose to use cotton fabrics that could be laundered.

4. **HOW WILL THE QUILT BE USED?** Since this quilt was destined for a silent auction, I didn't know how it would be used by the person with the winning bid. *Teal Beauty's* size and materials made it just as appropriate for a wall as it is for a bed or sofa.

5. **HOW BIG WILL THIS QUILT BE?** I wanted this quilt to be versatile and to have the widest appeal possible. I aimed for a size somewhere between a lap quilt and a twin quilt. This would be big enough to wrap up in, but not so big that it couldn't be hung on a wall.

6. **WHAT EFFECT DO YOU WANT TO ACHIEVE WITH THIS QUILT?** I wanted this quilt to be well constructed, well quilted, and beautiful. I wanted people to want to own it. I wanted people to bid big at the silent auction so that this quilt could bring in a large donation for cancer research.

7. **DO YOU HAVE SPECIFIC COLORS, SHAPES, PATTERNS IN MIND?** Teal is the color of ovarian cancer awareness. Our family had teal ribbons to wear and small collections of teal things we'd gathered as we all made this journey with my sister. The main color had to be teal.

When I started this project, I had no specific shapes or patterns in mind. Since I was working with a group of quilters, I needed a pattern that would produce consistently sized blocks regardless of the quilters' experience or skill. I also wanted a pattern that Vicki would have made. Loving mariner's compass and grandma's flower garden, she would not have opted for anything too simple. Foundation piecing seemed to be the obvious choice.

Teal Beauty by Cyndi Souder.
Courtesy of Nancy and Neil Weidner.

8. **WHAT ARTIFACTS DO YOU HAVE THAT YOU WANT TO INCLUDE?** I had many artifacts, but I did not want to use them for this project. Selfishly, I wanted to keep Vicki's things for myself rather than put them on a quilt that would probably be purchased by someone who had not known her.

9. **WHAT WILL YOU NEED TO ADD TO COMPLETE THIS QUILT?** To get this quilt done, I needed a pattern, more fabric, and a group of quilters ready to help. I also needed a venue where this quilt could be auctioned and the proceeds donated for cancer research.

10. **DESCRIBE THE QUILT. INCLUDE COLORS, MATERIALS, ANYTHING AND EVERYTHING YOU ARE CONSIDERING. FEEL FREE TO SKETCH.** At this point in the design process, I knew the quilt would be lap- to twin-sized and appropriate for use or hanging on a wall. I chose gold to complement the teal, and I knew that there would be a wide array of color values and variations. I also knew the design would be complex and that it would be foundation pieced by a group of quilters.

Teal Beauty and some of the quilters who helped make it. Standing left to right: Cyndi Souder, Beverly Burroughs, Kathy Lincoln, Karen Burshnick. Seated left to right: Diane Yim, Linda Cooper, Kathye Gillette, Linda Snow, and Libby Fritsche. A full list of names is on page 6.

WORKING WITH A GROUP: I believe in the power of quilters. I've never asked quilters for help and been refused. Whether you ask your bee, your guild, or an online group, sharing the work can make the difference between a good idea and a finished project. However, if you're going to work in a group, keep these tips in mind:

• Someone needs to be in charge to keep the group on course. Lead gently, but lead.

• Choose a pattern that everyone can sew. If you choose something complex, make sure your group is up for the challenge.

• Set a color palette and then graciously accept the fabric your friends offer you. However, be firm about your vision. If you are making a batik quilt, you may say no thank you to Civil War fabrics.

• Play to the strengths of the group. If you are lucky enough to have a longarmer who offers to do the quilting, accept the offer. If someone offers to prewash and press all of the fabric before cutting day, do a happy dance and hand over the yardage.

• Set a reasonable schedule. Quilters are busy people and we all work at different speeds. Communicate expectations and then be flexible.

• Thank everyone for their help. Writing your thank you note on a card with the project printed on the front makes a nice keepsake.

• Have fun!

The Design Process

DEVELOPING AN OVERALL DESIGN CONCEPT: Once I narrowed down the design concept, I shopped for existing patterns. I purchased *Japanese Fan* by Judy Niemeyer, a high-quality foundation piecing pattern. I think my sister would have approved.

With the color palette of teal and gold established, I was ready to move forward with construction.

The Construction Process

DEVELOPING A PLAN: I did not work on this project alone. My quilting friends were there during my sister's illness and they grieved with me when she was gone. As soon as I said I wanted to do something bigger than myself to commemorate her life, my friends asked how they could help.

I started slowly, pulling teal and gold batik fabrics from my sister's fabric stash. Then I moved to my own batik stash. Friends brought stacks of their own fabric for the project. The process was cathartic for all of us. I broadened the definitions of teal and gold to add range and interest to the color palette, shopping for additional fabric to fill in the holes.

As we collected fabric, I sent out a call for help to fellow members of my home guild. I also asked other quilting friends for help. Some of the quilters were experienced and proficient foundation piecers; others had never foundation pieced before, but were eager to learn so that they could help. In the end, twenty quilters pieced blocks for the quilt.

PIECING THE QUILT TOP: As the blocks began to arrive at my house, mail time became the highlight of my day. The fabrics were lovely, but the blocks were spectacular. I couldn't wait to put it all together!

I hung a large piece of felt on my quilt display stand and used this as a dedicated design wall. Blocks would arrive and up they would go onto the wall. I'd tinker with block placement and mix and match the completing corners and plain border pieces until I liked the overall effect. My friends would come over and play with the layout as well. When we were finally happy, I pieced the top, removing the foundation paper from behind each block.

QUILTING: I often send my larger quilts to one of my favorite longarm quilters. I call this "quilting by check." In this case, though, I felt I should do the quilting myself. Working on a domestic sewing machine, I quilted wavy flame-like lines radiating from the center of each circle. I aimed for a medium quilting density that would enhance but not upstage the overall design.

PERSONALIZING THE LABEL: Labels are important for all quilts, but I agonized over the label for this project. Since the quilt was to be auctioned at a fundraiser, I correctly assumed that I would not know the new owners. I also figured that the new owners would not necessarily be interested in seeing all of the information I wanted to include on the label.

To create the label, I printed the text on printer-ready fabric. I then bordered the label and added a backing that coordinated with the quilt back. I used the pillowcase technique to stitch and turn the label so that the edges were neatly encased, adding a ribbon loop at one corner.

Once the label was pressed, I folded it to look like an envelope with the printed information on the inside. A search through my button collection yielded a silver button with a starburst pattern reminiscent of the quilt pattern. If I remember correctly, I bought this button on a sewing trip with my sister. It seemed right to include it here. The loop goes around the button and keeps the label attractively closed.

NAMING THE QUILT: From the beginning, I knew this quilt would be called "Teal Beauty." I wanted to use the word "teal" to highlight the ovarian cancer connection to this quilt. I also liked the fact that this pattern is a play on the traditional New York Beauty block. My sister's daughter Karen lived in New York for a while and I thought of her as my New York Beauty. Combined, "Teal Beauty" seemed like an appropriate title.

Details of *Teal Beauty* by Cyndi Souder.
Courtesy of Nancy and Neil Weidner.

The Quilt's Future

My husband and I delivered the completed quilt to London for a black-tie gala fundraiser my niece had planned. The quilt had been appraised for $3,500; I hoped it would raise at least that much. Inside the main hall of the Imperial War Museum, I was overwhelmed at the quality and quantity of the auction items. There was only one quilt, and I hoped it would hold its own against the treasures and extravagant luxuries on the silent auction tables.

At the end of the evening, we learned that *Teal Beauty* brought in the second largest donation of the night at £4,500 ($9,000)! Proceeds from *Teal Beauty* went to the Institute of Cancer Research (ICR), a world leader in cancer research.

Call to Action: Fundraising, Charity, and Service quilts

If you feel strongly about supporting a charity or an organization, put your quilting skills to work for the cause. Work alone or invite your quilting friends to join you.

Just be sure to contact the organization first to confirm that they can use your quilt. Before *Teal Beauty*, I offered a quilt to a cancer awareness group near my home with the expectation that they would use it as a fundraiser. They did not want a quilt; they wanted a check. Any check I could have given them would have been much smaller than the $9,000 donated to the Institute for Cancer Research for *Teal Beauty*. I'm glad I did a little research before I started sewing.

I've included a list of organizations who might appreciate your help in the Resources section on page 80.

I believe that every baby deserves a baby quilt. Coming into this world is a big deal and we should all celebrate it. This strippy baby quilt was born from a roll of lovely precut batiks without the use of a pattern. Sometimes when you're working with beautiful fabrics, you don't need a pattern. Simply sewing strips together can be a lovely way to piece a quilt top.

Worksheet for Strippy Baby Quilt

1. **WHAT OR WHOM WILL THIS QUILT COMMEMORATE?** This strippy baby quilt was designed to welcome the first child of our new neighbors.

2. **DESCRIBE THE PERSON, LIFE, OR EVENT YOU ARE COMMEMORATING.** If you're making a baby quilt, you're commemorating the baby, but you're designing the quilt for the parents. These parents had recently moved into our neighborhood of contemporary homes. They enjoy outdoor activities, attended the same university, and are ice hockey fans. She is from Canada. We like them both very much.

3. **DESCRIBE THE QUILT'S ENVIRONMENT.** Baby quilts are destined for wear and tear. I planned to use fabrics that would stand up to repeated spills and laundry.

4. **HOW WILL THE QUILT BE USED?** Baby quilts are generally utility quilts. I expected this quilt to be used heavily.

5. **HOW BIG WILL THIS QUILT BE?** I try to keep baby quilt sizes small enough to use the standard width of fabric as a backing without having to piece it. Generally, this means the quilt would be 42" wide or less. It depends on the backing fabric.

6. **WHAT EFFECT DO YOU WANT TO ACHIEVE WITH THIS QUILT?** I wanted the parents to be happy with the new quilt. I was aiming for simple, calm, and well-constructed.

7. **DO YOU HAVE SPECIFIC COLORS, SHAPES, PATTERNS IN MIND?** In planning this quilt, I had no specific information about the gender of the baby or the decorating scheme of the nursery. I planned to use gender-neutral colors in a simple design.

8. **WHAT ARTIFACTS DO YOU HAVE THAT YOU WANT TO INCLUDE?** Because this is a utility quilt for a baby, I did not plan to use any artifacts.

9. **WHAT WILL YOU NEED TO ADD TO COMPLETE THIS QUILT?** I needed fabric and a design. I also needed to choose a color palette.

10. **DESCRIBE THE QUILT. INCLUDE COLORS, MATERIALS, ANYTHING, AND EVERYTHING YOU ARE CONSIDERING. FEEL FREE TO SKETCH.** At this point, I didn't know much. The quilt would be a cotton baby quilt, 42" wide or less, in gender-neutral colors.

Strippy Baby Quilt by Cyndi Souder.

Strips laid out to sew for the
Strippy Baby Quilt.

Batik Rail Fence by Cyndi Souder.

The Design Process

DEVELOPING AN OVERALL DESIGN CONCEPT: I designed this baby quilt as I walked a quilt show with a quilting friend. When I visited my favorite batik vendor and saw his Tiki Rolls of 2-1/2" precut batik strips, I knew I wanted to use them.

At first, I resisted the many enticing precut selections of fabric. It seemed like every fabric manufacturer offered them and I wanted to choose my own fabric combinations. Yes, I was stubborn. Eventually, I bought a pack of Bali Pops and made them into a clothesline bag without even pausing to rearrange the order of the strips. I was hooked.

A few thoughts about precut fabric packets:

• The fabrics in each packet are selected to coordinate, saving you shopping time and occasionally pushing you outside of your comfort zone with fabrics you might not have chosen.

• The fabrics are precut, saving you cutting time if you have a pattern in mind that uses those precut sizes. Luckily, designers are now creating patterns specifically for these precut fabrics. Precuts have become easy to use.

• Precuts are not prewashed. If you want to prewash your fabric (and I generally do), you may lose some size to shrinkage or frayed edges. Washing precut fabric in lingerie or laundry bags can help protect them from fraying.

The Construction Process

DEVELOPING A PLAN: Because of their size, baby quilts are great for trying out new ideas and techniques. In this case, I wanted to try just sewing the strips together side by side into a strippy panel. I decided to leave the strips in the order in which they were packaged — or at least I'd try. There were too many strips to use them all in this one quilt top, and so I knew I'd set some of the strips aside.

PIECING THE QUILT TOP: I chose to use a symmetrical layout, starting in the center and moving toward the ends. I laid out the strips, did a tiny bit of rearranging, and sewed the strips together. Once I decided how big the finished quilt would be, I trimmed the pieced center section down to size. For this quilt, I trimmed the center section to 32" wide by 42" high.

I chose a purple/lavender batik from my fabric stash to complete the top and decided I needed a stopper border between the pieced center and the lavender border. I chose a very pale apricot/yellow for contrast and cut it into 1" wide strips. I cut the lavender into 3-1/2" wide strips for the outer border.

STOPPER BORDERS: Stopper borders are skinny borders designed to "stop" the colors and patterns in the center section from visually flowing into the outer border.

In this quilt, the printed purple strips are very close in color and value to the outer border. If there were no light stopper border, those purple strips would look too similar to the outer border and would appear to be connected to it or made from the same fabric. The stopper border in this quilt clearly separates the pieced center from the outer border and gives a nice crisp appearance.

I stitched the light stopper border first to the long sides of the pieced center section and then to the ends. I repeated the process with the lavender outer border.

QUILTING: Because I was working on deadline and the quilt is a reasonably small size, I did the machine quilting myself.

• The first quilting I did on this baby quilt was to stitch in the ditch on both sides of the skinny stopper border. I did not quilt inside the stopper border.

• Then, I machine quilted the pieced center with a meander pattern using multi-colored variegated thread.

• I machine quilted a meander pattern on the outer border using lavender and purple variegated thread.

• I used the same bobbin thread for all parts of the quilt so that the back of the quilt would look consistent.

PERSONALIZING THE LABEL: Labels for baby quilts are tricky. It's all about timing. If you can wait until the baby is born, then you can add a label before you give away your quilt. If you are presenting the quilt before the baby is born, you don't have any real information to put on the label other than your own name. You can always make the label after the baby is born and then sew the label on while you visit with the new parents.

I don't recommend sending a label with the expectation that the family will sew it on. They'll be busy and that's part of your gift. Keep the label and sew it on yourself when you visit the baby.

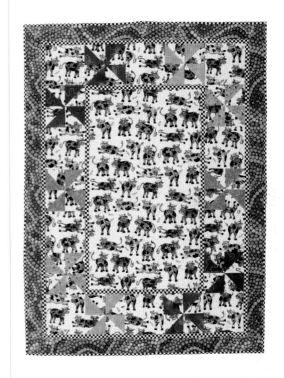

Andrew's Baby Quilt by Cyndi Souder. *Courtesy of Andrew Greve.*

Draft label from *Andrew's Baby Quilt* by Cyndi Souder. Notice the quilt blocks in front of the cow appear in the finished quilt. Andrew received the quilt and the stuffed cow together.

Quilts that Start with an Idea

Sometimes a quilt design begins with a concept. If we're lucky, we also have some clothing or fabric to work with. Using the worksheet helps to flesh out the concept and make design decisions.

This was the case with Mentor, Guru and Sage. My client came to me with a bunch of bowties and the memory of an insightful and intelligent man with a wonderful sense of decency and humor devoted to museums and the art world. As I spoke with the client and later completed the worksheet, the quilt design took shape.

Worksheet for Mentor, Guru and Sage

1. **WHAT OR WHOM WILL THIS QUILT COMMEMORATE?** My client's late husband, Steve Weil, spent twenty-two years as Deputy Director of the Hirshhorn Museum and Sculpture Garden in Washington, DC, the Smithsonian's museum of modern and contemporary art. This Celebration Quilt was meant to honor his personality and his life in a way that was appropriate to his passion for art and museums.

2. **DESCRIBE THE PERSON, LIFE, OR EVENT YOU ARE COMMEMORATING.** Steve was a strong presence in the museum world. He believed museums should serve their communities and was committed to education and leadership. His colleagues thought of him as a mentor, a guru, and a sage. He wore a bow tie to work every day, amassing a huge collection of them from gifts and travel. He had a quick wit and collected pithy quotes on a bulletin board in his office.

3. **DESCRIBE THE QUILT'S ENVIRONMENT.** Originally, my client wanted the quilt to cover her bed but not hang over the sides. Once I realized there were small dogs in her home, I convinced her to consider hanging the quilt on the wall where it could be appreciated without the threat of damage or dog hair. Ultimately, the quilt was designed to hang above the head of her bed.

4. **HOW WILL THE QUILT BE USED?** The quilt was designed to be a wall quilt to hang without a frame. To avoid distracting hardware, we decided to hang it using a flat wooden slat hidden inside a hanging sleeve. The hanging system is not visible from the front of the quilt.

5. **HOW BIG WILL THIS QUILT BE?** This number was a moving target in this project's planning stage. When we started planning, we worked with 50" wide by 65" high. When we completed the planning stage, we agreed on 70" wide by 40" high. The wider dimension aligned the quilt width with the bed width, creating a more balanced look. The shorter height allowed for enough empty wall space above the pillows on the bed so the quilt would not look crowded into the available space.

6. **WHAT EFFECT DO YOU WANT TO ACHIEVE WITH THIS QUILT?** I have to admit that designing this quilt was intimidating. Steve Weil was an important man in the museum world and my client wanted this Celebration Quilt to be in line with his position. In my mind, that meant the quilt needed to be "arty" enough but not stuffy. The challenge was this: How would I make a serious art quilt that clearly communicates a sense of energy and humor?

7. **DO YOU HAVE SPECIFIC COLORS, SHAPES, PATTERNS IN MIND?** My client was in the midst of renovating her home, including her bedroom where the quilt would be hung. The flooring had been done with bow-tie inserts in mahogany.

Mentor, Guru and Sage by Cyndi Souder. *Photograph by Thom Goertel. Courtesy of Wendy Luke.*

She had mahogany plantation shutters and the walls were painted white with peach undertones. The room was filled with art, which she had professionally rehung to accommodate the new Celebration Quilt. In her words, the room could take a bold statement.

8. **WHAT ARTIFACTS DO YOU HAVE THAT YOU WANT TO INCLUDE?** This is always the most interesting part of the design process for me. What do I have to work with? My client brought me her late husband's signature bow ties – 166 of them! She also wanted me to include quotes from his bulletin board and a cartoon that had been drawn of him. And so I had tiny bits of fabric, lots of text, and a line drawing that had to be reproduced well enough to be recognizable.

9. **WHAT WILL YOU NEED TO ADD TO COMPLETE THIS QUILT?** In a word: structure. I needed fabric for the background, backing, and binding. I also needed a concept that could combine the ties, the quotes, and the cartoon in a way that would create the energy and the importance that the quilt needed to convey.

10. **DESCRIBE THE QUILT. INCLUDE COLORS, MATERIALS, ANYTHING, AND EVERYTHING YOU ARE CONSIDERING. FEEL FREE TO SKETCH.** At this point, I don't have a concrete design. I know that the quilt will have many colors because of the bow ties. I know that I can go big and bold with the design, but the details will be important, too.

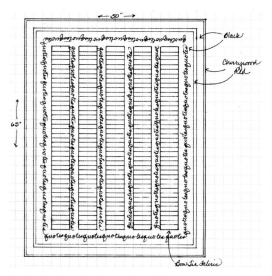

Design option 1 for *Mentor, Guru and Sage.*

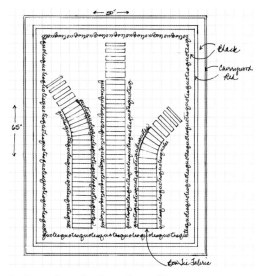

Design option 2 for *Mentor, Guru and Sage.*

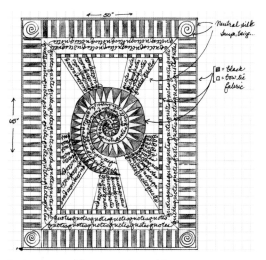

Design option 3 for *Mentor, Guru and Sage.*

The Design Process

Before I met this client in person, I knew she had a collection of bowties she wanted me to use. That's all I knew. My first thought was to use the bow ties in a traditional bow tie block. Looking back, I'm surprised I didn't lose all standing in my client's eyes with that uninspired concept. Knowing what I now know about her late husband, this first try was unimaginative and too much of a pun.

After I learned more about Steve Weil, I returned to the materials *(see #8 on the worksheet)* and started again. My thoughts, in no particular order:

• I had a lot of small pieces of really interesting fabric.
• I wanted to use as many different pieces of bow tie fabric as I could.
• The bowtie fabric would be the primary visual element for the quilt.
• I needed to incorporate lots of writing, but the writing would not be the focal point.
• I had to find a way to recreate the cartoon as a recognizable feature.

DESIGN OPTIONS: I wanted to find a traditional pattern that could serve as a starting point for this art quilt. What traditional pattern would showcase lots of small pieces of fabric without looking too scrappy? I could have gone in a number of different directions — crazy quilt, charm quilt, postage stamp quilt — but none of these ideas felt right. I kept coming back to the Chinese coin pattern. This would allow me to use lots of small strips of different fabrics with one background fabric to pull it all together. I could include the quotes by QuiltWriting on each side of the coin stacks and around the edges. I had no place for the cartoon yet, but I decided to use this as Option One. At this point in the planning, the dimensions were still the original 50" wide by 65" high.

For Option Two, I changed the design from five stacks to three stacks and bent the outside stacks out toward the edges. The angles gave me a spot for the cartoon. Then I took the coins at the top of the outside stacks and pulled them up and away from each other, creating the illusion that the tops were coming off the stacks. I thought that added some movement and interest. Again, I added QuiltWriting around the stacks and the edges.

For Option Three, I wanted to really push the artistic aspect of the quilt. Because of the recurring circles in the structure of the Hirshhorn, I wanted to incorporate circles into a design option. I had recently purchased a book about spirals and I was captivated by the idea of using them in this quilt.

The finished quilt was based on the second design option, but with some changes.

• By this time, we had adjusted our size to the final 70" wide by 40" high.
• We decided to fill the extra width by creating five stacks rather than three.
• We added small square confetti coming out of the top of each stack for additional energy and movement.
• We added an extra round of QuiltWriting on the outside of the skinny red border, allowing more room for additional quotes.
• We decided the quotes would be separated by a small quilted bow tie shape.

• We determined the Art Law cartoon would be stitched into the upper right corner.

To construct the quilt, I added black Dupioni silk for the background and red silk for the skinny border. All of the other fabric comes from the bow ties.

The Construction Process

DEVELOPING A PLAN: Once the design was established, I needed to figure out how to construct the quilt. Developing a plan is just a problem-solving exercise and shouldn't be intimidating or scary. This is the phase where you get to use all of the classes you've taken, all of the books you've read, and all of the quilting experience you have. Your quilting toolbox is better stocked than you may think.

For *Mentor, Guru and Sage*, there were challenges:

• How should I go about creating the pattern?
• How would I "free" the most fabric I could get from each bowtie?
• Once the bow ties were ripped apart, how would I use the fabric? What would go where?
• Would the variety of bow tie fabric, including silk, wool, polyester, and cotton, present any special problems?
• Which quotes would I use on the quilt? There were too many to use them all!
• What was the best way to add the "Art Law" cartoon to the quilt?

CREATING A PATTERN: For this quilt, I needed to create a pattern. Taking into consideration the overall size of the quilt and the unstable bowtie fabrics, I decided to foundation piece the quilt top, which allowed me to piece one section at a time and then sew them together once all of the sections were completed. Foundation piecing also provided extra stability where the bowtie fabric would be used.

I followed these straightforward steps:

1. I projected the full-size design onto a wall and traced it onto a very large piece of paper.
2. I added a few additional lines to aid in construction and traced over all lines with a bold marker.
3. I numbered the sections and added ticks or hash marks so that I could easily match the seams when it came time to reassemble the pieces.
4. Using muslin and a fabric marker, I traced each section of the design onto a separate piece of fabric, transferring all numbers and marks.

PIECING THE QUILT TOP: Before I could piece the top, I had to come up with a plan for how to arrange the bowtie fabrics. I didn't want the quilt to look random or scrappy, so I decided to group colors together and then work from dark to light wherever I had enough of the right tie fabrics. To make this work, I needed to assess what bow tie fabrics I had. At this point, the ties had all been dry cleaned and ripped apart. I laid out all of the bow tie pieces, sorting them by color.

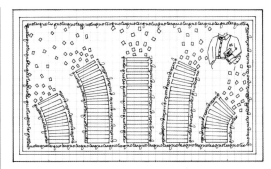

Final design for *Mentor, Guru and Sage*.

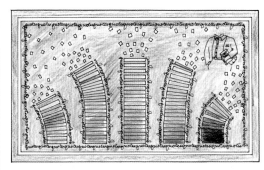

Final design with color for *Mentor, Guru and Sage*.

Getting into the Zone:

I did not know Steve Weil, which put me at a disadvantage when it came time to infuse this quilt with his spirit and personality. To help me become better acquainted with her late husband, my client brought me CDs from his extensive music collection. I was thrilled to see Miles Davis in the mix and listened to his music as I worked on Mentor, Guru and Sage. I find that listening to the same music each time I work on a piece helps me get into the zone more quickly when I've had to spend some time away from the studio.

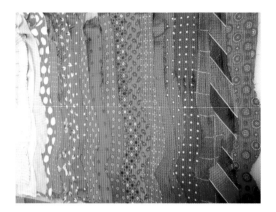

Red bowties, ripped.

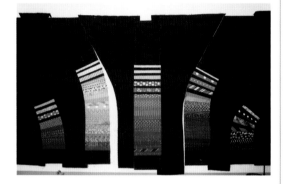

Mentor, Guru and Sage under construction on the design wall.

Example of QuiltWriting on *Mentor, Guru and Sage.*

Quilted cartoon on *Mentor, Guru and Sage* by Cyndi Souder.
Photograph by Thom Goertel. Courtesy of Wendy Luke.

I pieced each "stack" by laying out the bow tie fabric according to plan and sewing them directly onto the fabric foundation. Anything not covered by bowtie fabric was considered background and I added the black Dupioni silk to those areas.

I then covered the remaining foundation pieces with the black silk to create the background, using a slightly longer stitch just outside the seam lines. Once all of the foundation fabric was covered with background silk or bow tie fabric, I used the tick marks on the foundation to sew the stacks and background pieces together into one panel.

Finally, I trimmed the edges and added the narrow red border followed by a wider black border.

QUILTING, QUILTWRITING, AND A CARTOON: The first quilting I did was ditchwork (stitching in the ditch) with black thread. I wanted to anchor the layers together and ensure that the smooth, straight edges of the stacks and borders would remain smooth and straight.

QuiltWriting was next. My client sent me a file with all of the quotes she wanted me to use listed in order of priority. For detailed instructions on how to lay out words for QuiltWriting, see Quilting Tips on **page 57**. Changing to taupe thread, I stitched the quotes into the quilt.

After the QuiltWriting was completed, I stitched in the "Art Law" cartoon. To do this, I traced the cartoon onto thin paper and stitched right through the paper. For more detailed instructions on how to do this, see Quilting Tips **page 60**.

PERSONALIZING THE LABEL: No quilt is complete without a label. Working with my client, we drafted the text and chose an image for the label.

NAMING THE QUILT: For fun, my client and her husband used to create names for mythical law firms. Sometimes they were funny and sometimes they were clever. One of these names was "Mentor, Guru and Sage." My client tells me her husband was all of those things. In her chosen field, she is a sage and often a mentor. This title was perfect for her quilt.

The Quilt's Future

Some Celebration Quilts are quick to make and will be used until they are worn out. Others are destined to be treated as art and will outlive their owners. Soon after my client received this quilt, we talked about what plans she might make for the quilt's future. There were three grown children to consider as well as some discussion about donating it to a museum. Ultimately, she will probably leave the quilt to the children as part of her estate. For the short run, my client asked me to make three smaller quilts — we called them quiltlets — for the children to enjoy now. Using leftover bowtie fabric and silk, I made three scaled-down versions of *Mentor, Guru and Sage.* All three quilts were roughly the same and featured the same quotes along the bottom.

Mentor, Guru and Sage

A bow-tie quilt in honor of --

Stephen E. Weil
June 24, 1928 – August 9, 2005

An innovative thinker and provocateur in the museum world.
Steve profoundly loved and was loved by his wife, Wendy Luke.
He was a proud father of three remarkable children and an awed grandfather.
He was a renaissance man, wise, decent, very funny, and an enthusiastic bow tie wearer.

Cyndi Souder 2007 www.MoonlightingQuilts.com

Label for *Mentor, Guru and Sage* by Cyndi Souder.

Mentor, Guru and Sage Quiltlet by Cyndi Souder.
Photograph by Yoni Weil. Courtesy of David Weil.

Mentor, Guru and Sage Quiltlets by Cyndi Souder.

My brother-in-law, John Souder, has been involved in the World Championship Punkin Chunkin for as long as I can remember. He looks forward to it every year and participates fully. When I drew John's name for Christmas one year, I knew I wanted to make him a quilt that would be personal to him and that would commemorate his fascination with the Punkin Chunkin. I also knew this quilt would include a few tee shirts, and I felt it would be appropriate to use a traditional pattern.

Worksheet for Flying Pumpkins

1. **WHAT OR WHOM WILL THIS QUILT COMMEMORATE?** *Flying Pumpkins* was designed to celebrate my brother-in-law's involvement and love affair with the Delaware phenomenon called the World Championship Punkin Chunkin. Technically, this quilt commemorates my brother-in-law and the Punkin Chunkin.

2. **DESCRIBE THE PERSON, LIFE, OR EVENT YOU ARE COMMEMORATING.** The Punkin Chunkin is a competition where people build contraptions to hurl pumpkins as far as possible. The current record is nearly a mile! The event started in 1986 and my brother-in-law has been involved in some capacity almost every year since then.

   John is a master electrician, small business owner, Punkin Chunkin aficionado, and exactly the person you want to have around if disaster strikes.

3. **DESCRIBE THE QUILT'S ENVIRONMENT.** I planned for this to be a utility quilt. John sets up his camper at the Punkin Chunkin to minimize his time in traffic and to allow himself time to socialize after hours. I expected him to use the quilt in the camper and so I used cotton fabrics that could be laundered.

4. **HOW WILL THE QUILT BE USED?** I expected this quilt to be used in the camper and possibly at John's home. It was designed to be a utility quilt.

5. **HOW BIG WILL THIS QUILT BE?** I wanted this quilt to be large enough to be useful. I measured the mattress in the camper to ensure the quilt would more than cover it.

6. **WHAT EFFECT DO YOU WANT TO ACHIEVE WITH THIS QUILT?** I wanted this quilt to be 100% pumpkin. I also wanted it to be personal for John. If possible, I wanted the quilt to include tee shirts, but I wanted the tee shirts to be integrated into the overall design rather than it dominating.

7. **DO YOU HAVE SPECIFIC COLORS, SHAPES, PATTERNS IN MIND?** The Punkin Chunkin is held each year on the weekend after Halloween. I planned to use Halloween colors, building the color palette around orange and black.

8. **WHAT ARTIFACTS DO YOU HAVE THAT YOU WANT TO INCLUDE?** Throughout his time with the Punkin Chunkin, John has collected tee shirts. When I told him I wanted to make this quilt for him, I asked him for tee shirts he wanted to include in the quilt. He gave me three: the annual Punkin Chunkin shirt from 2005, the 1998 Hypertension III team shirt, and the 1996 Loaded Boing team shirt, which includes a cartoon of him in the graphic.

9. **WHAT WILL YOU NEED TO ADD TO COMPLETE THIS QUILT?** Three tee shirts and a Halloween color palette would not be enough to create a quilt. I would need a collection of fabrics and ideas for design and layout.

Flying Pumpkins by Cyndi Souder.
Courtesy of John R. Souder.

49 *Forever!* by Kathy Lincoln. These nine-patch blocks were made by Kathy's friends to celebrate a milestone birthday. *Courtesy of the artist.*

10. Describe the quilt. Include colors, materials, anything and everything you are considering. Feel free to sketch. I knew the quilt would be predominately orange and black. It would include three tee shirts and be large enough to cover the mattress in John's camper.

The Design Process

Developing an Overall Design Concept: I hunted through my fabric stash and the local quilt shop for Halloween fabric, specifically fabric with pumpkins. Since I wanted to use black for some solid blocks, I also looked for a black fabric with a subtle design.

I decided to use the fun Halloween fabrics to create nine-patch blocks that would alternate with the plain black blocks. I would cut the tee shirts into blocks that would fit in with this plan. Because the tee shirt designs were not the same size as the 9" blocks, I knew I would need to make adjustments as I worked.

If I were using only nine-patch and solid alternating blocks, I'd need twenty-four of each for a total of forty-eight blocks. The layout would be six rows and eight columns.

The Construction Process

Piecing the Quilt Top: Piecing the top went pretty quickly despite the fact that I did not strip-piece the nine-patch blocks.

- **Tee Shirts –** Before I cut the fronts of the tee shirts to size, I removed the collars, sleeves, and backs and then stabilized the fronts by fusing a woven interfacing to the wrong side of the tee shirt. If I hadn't stabilized the fabric, the tee shirt knit was likely to stretch out of shape and curl around the edges. For more information about working with difficult fabrics, read **page 49**.

Once the tee shirt fronts were stable, I measured the design and determined that the finished size would be based on the 3-6-9 principle. I tried to center the design within those measurements, added a half-inch seam allowance, and cut the pieces. The Hypertension III tee was not quite wide enough to cut 15", and 12" would have cropped part of the design. To work around this measurement, I waited until I knew where the tee shirt block would go and added the necessary filler strips.

- **Solid Blocks –** I cut 24 solid blocks to 9-1/2" (9" finished size) and set them aside.

- **Nine-Patch Blocks –** According to my plan, I expected to need 24 nine-patch blocks, but I actually used 22. I used tee shirts where two of the nine-patches would have gone. If I had sketched this quilt before layout, I would have known exactly how many full blocks I needed, but I wanted to make the blocks first and then play with the layout.

The Benefits of Using Traditional Blocks

Most of the quilters I know began their quilting lives as traditional quilters. My first pieced quilt was a log cabin, which is a block I still love. If you have a favorite traditional block, then you may already have quick piecing techniques and any special tools you may need to construct it. In addition, many traditional blocks are simple to resize. If you use Electric Quilt®, you can easily lay out your quilt design and play with the many traditional blocks that are included with the program. Finally, if you want your quilt to have a traditional feel, then using traditional blocks will help you achieve that goal.

THE 3-6-9 PRINCIPLE: Piecing a quilt is like putting together a puzzle, but with puzzles you know the pieces will all fit together. With quilts, it takes planning for all of the pieces to fit.

When I'm working without a pattern, I sometimes use the 3-6-9 principle. Blocks with finished sizes of 3", 6", and 9" will all fit together. You could extend this to 12" and other numbers that are divisible by three, but I usually stick to 3", 6", and 9". Remember, this measurement is the finished size, so your cut size will be a half-inch larger to accommodate quarter-inch seam allowances. For a 6" block, you'd cut a 6-1/2" square.

You can use this design principle when you're planning a quilt for yourself or if you're working with a group. One of my professional groups honors a different member each year at our annual conference. Each year, we all bring in blocks that follow the 3-6-9 principle. The honoree can easily add whatever filler blocks and strips she needs to complete her new quilt top without any difficult math or pattern drafting.

If all of the nine-patch blocks were to be made of the same fabrics, I would have strip-pieced them. However, I had only enough of most fabric combinations to make two blocks each. I cut the nine-patch fabrics into 3-1/2" squares (3" finished size) and then constructed the blocks square by square.

At the layout stage, I removed parts of the nine-patch blocks to accommodate the irregular tee shirt block sizes. Yes, this meant ripping, but it seemed faster to do it this way than it would have been to draft the quilt ahead of time. This method also allowed me to move the full blocks around to play with the layout before I committed to which blocks would become partial blocks.

- **STOPPER BORDER** – Since the outer border fabric I chose was busy with lots of color and variations, I wanted to add a small border that would separate the pieced center section from the other border. I choose to use one of the more subdued fabrics from the nine-patch blocks. I cut the stopper border to 2" strips (1-1/2" finished size) and stitched it first to the long sides of the quilt and then to the shorter ends. For more information about stopper borders, read **page 29**.

- **OUTER BORDER** – For the outer border, I wanted a fabric that echoed the colors and energy of the pieced center of the quilt. I cut 4-3/4" strips (4-1/4" finished size) and stitched it first to the long sides of the quilt and then to the shorter ends.

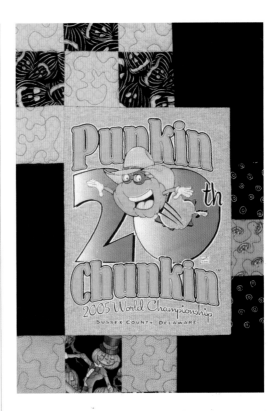

Detail of *Flying Pumpkins* by Cyndi Souder. *Courtesy of John R. Souder.*

QUILTING: While I often send bed-sized quilts to my favorite longarm quilters, I decided to quilt Flying Pumpkins myself. This may have had something to do with a deadline. I promised this quilt as a holiday present to John; the delivery of the quilt had to be in time for that year's Punkin Chunkin right after Halloween.

I used black thread for all of the quilting on Flying Pumpkins. I used piecing-weight thread because a heavier quilting-weight thread could have distracted from the fabrics.

- **STITCH IN THE DITCH** – The first quilting I did on this project was to stitch in the ditch around both sides of the narrow stopper border. This anchors the quilt layers and keeps those straight lines looking crisp and straight. Then I stitched in the ditch around each of the tee shirt blocks for additional stability.

- **GENERAL FREE MOTION QUILTING** – Next, I quilted a medium-sized meander all over the outer border and the center panel, saving the tee shirt blocks for special treatment.

- **PERSONALIZED FREE MOTION QUILTING** – For the tee shirt blocks, I quilted around the words and the big shapes to anchor the layers of the quilt together. I also chose shapes and features that I wanted to highlight and quilted around them.

- **QUILTWRITING** – I signed my quilt in the stopper border by QuiltWriting my name. You can't see it from the front, but it's there.

PERSONALIZING THE LABEL: To create the label, I printed the text on printer-ready fabric. I bordered the label with fabric from the stopper border. I like to repeat fabrics from the front of my quilts on the back.

NAMING THE QUILT: Naming this quilt "Flying Pumpkins" took me back to when I first attended the Punkin Chunkin. I expected to see a bunch of guys out in the middle of a field fiddling with rickety homemade pumpkin-throwing machines. Boy was I wrong! What I saw was a variety of catapults, trebuchets, and other contraptions built and operated by boys and girls, men and women. The biggest surprise for me was the air cannon with laser-guided targeting. These competitors take their Punkin Chunkin seriously. When the pumpkin leaves the barrel of an air cannon, it disappears in a hurry. Some might even say the pumpkins fly.

Label from *Flying Pumpkins* by Cyndi Souder.
Courtesy of John R. Souder.

Are Your Quilts Colorfast?

With today's textile technology, we'd like to think that all of our beautiful fabrics are colorfast. Unfortunately, that's not always the case. Color bleeding comes from some pretty unexpected places. I expect red to run, but cobalt blue can be unstable and so can any other highly saturated color.

I prewash my fabrics in loads sorted by color. Sometimes a piece of fabric gets through this process without my noticing the color transfer. The label on Flying Pumpkins was printed on white printer-ready fabric and it was white when I presented it to John. I laundered the quilt by itself and, as you can see, now the label is certainly not white. No other fabric in the quilt was affected.

If I had expected color bleeding to be a problem, I would have prevented it by using Synthrapol® to bond with the excess color and wash it out or Shout Color Catchers® to trap the excess color to prevent bleeding onto other fabrics. It's better to be safe and use the appropriate products when you're working with bright or saturated colors.

Quilts Designed around Artifacts

Worksheet for Too Much Soul to Control

1. **WHAT OR WHOM WILL THIS QUILT COMMEMORATE?** My client wanted to pay tribute to her late husband, Michael Kaye. When he died at age 55, less than three weeks after a sudden hospitalization, she vowed she would find a way to honor the man who had been her husband, her colleague, and her best friend.

2. **DESCRIBE THE PERSON, LIFE, OR EVENT YOU ARE COMMEMORATING.** From the moment my client began to tell me about her husband, I knew this man had been larger than life. Born and raised in South Philadelphia, Michael had been smart, funny, generous, and charismatic. He had a wealth of friends and lived passionately through his many interests and activities. Luckily for me, he also loved clothes. Because of that, I had a lot of raw material – clothing and accessories – to work with.

3. **DESCRIBE THE QUILT'S ENVIRONMENT.** My client wanted the quilt for her bedroom wall. She created a special wall area to highlight the quilt so that she could enjoy it every day. The walls in her bedroom were off white. The room included contemporary bamboo furniture, black lacquer framed artwork, and highlights of Chinese red and gold leaf.

4. **HOW WILL THE QUILT BE USED?** *Too Much Soul to Control* was designed to be a wall quilt. We originally planned to frame it in a Plexiglas® box frame, but later realized that the frame would create an unnecessary visual and tactile barrier, especially if my client wanted access to any of the artifacts included on the quilt.

5. **HOW BIG WILL THIS QUILT BE?** The finished quilt was 36" square. The size was limited by the wall on which the client planned to hang her quilt.

6. **WHAT EFFECT DO YOU WANT TO ACHIEVE WITH THIS QUILT?** My client and I both wanted to infuse as much of Michael's spirit and energy as possible into the quilt. With that in mind, I wanted a design that showed movement and wasn't static or too symmetrical. I wanted to use color and a variety of artifacts, but I didn't want the quilt to look scrappy or cluttered. I wanted Michael's friends to see the quilt and recognize him in it.

7. **DO YOU HAVE SPECIFIC COLORS, SHAPES, OR PATTERNS IN MIND?** This was one of the most challenging design tasks I've had. I considered and discarded myriad traditional and contemporary patterns. After meeting with my client and reviewing my notes, there were no obvious solutions.

8. **WHAT ARTIFACTS DO YOU HAVE THAT YOU WANT TO INCLUDE?** Oh, I had bags and bags of shirts, socks, and ties. I had Hawaiian shirts still on hangers from the dry cleaners. My client brought me her husband's Lanvin tuxedo and insisted

For Mentor, Guru and Sage (page 30), I had only bowties, a collection of quotes, and a cartoon for physical artifacts. For Too Much Soul to Control, I had a bounty of material. In fact, I was a bit overwhelmed by the sheer volume of items my client brought me. In the end, I was happy to have so many choices. Without the broad array of treasures and personal effects, we would not have been able to capture Michael's essence.

I include it, since she had such happy memories of him when he wore it. She also brought a collection of photographs, jewelry, accessories, recipes, eulogies, and e-mail. She even brought me their wedding vows. While the sheer volume of materials was overwhelming, I'd rather have too much than too little to work with.

9. **WHAT WILL YOU NEED TO ADD TO COMPLETE THIS QUILT?** In short, I needed a unifying concept. Until I had a design concept, I couldn't begin to decide what more I would need to complete this quilt. At the very least, I needed some sort of fabric that would unify the many disparate elements. Beyond that, I needed inspiration. In the end, I only added black fabric. Everything else came from my client.

10. **DESCRIBE THE QUILT. INCLUDE COLORS, MATERIALS, ANYTHING, AND EVERYTHING YOU ARE CONSIDERING. FEEL FREE TO SKETCH.** Until inspiration struck, I could not "see" the quilt. I knew it would be 36" square and that it would include the tuxedo. At my client's request, the quilt would also include her husband's Marilyn Monroe watch and suspenders, a few tee shirts, and fabric from at least one Hawaiian shirt. I knew my client wanted some words included and liked my QuiltWriting technique. I planned to include some key phrases and words from various sources.

The Design Process

DEVELOPING AN OVERALL DESIGN CONCEPT: I usually like to present my clients with two or three design options. In this case, however, I was so confident that my first solid design idea was the right one for this quilt that I sent only one option in my proposal. If my client had reservations, I would simply start again.

The overall unifying theme of the quilt came from a conversation I had with my client. She and her husband loved films. They would watch movies for hours — talking about them, enjoying them, and sharing them. It occurred to me that I could use the visual aspect of film frames to show different facets of Michael's personality. The film would visually unify the many different things I needed to incorporate into this quilt!

DESIGNING AROUND THE ARTIFACTS: With my client's quick and happy approval, it was time to get to work. In the initial design, I'd listed some of the artifacts that were particularly important to include. However, this was a working sketch in need of details. Working larger, I sketched again, this time to scale. I listed everything we wanted to include in the quilt and tried to assign places for each item, including all of the words.

Fitting everything into this relatively small quilt was going to be a challenge. I needed to find the balance between the art needed to make all of these different elements look good together and the engineering necessary to make the quilt hang flat under the uneven weight.

Design sketch for *Too Much Soul to Control* by Cyndi Souder.

Too Much Soul to Control by Cyndi Souder.
Courtesy of Linda Lee Kaye.

The Construction Process

DEVELOPING A PLAN: Once I had a working sketch, I couldn't wait to get started. There would be a few construction challenges, but the plan seemed pretty simple. I would work on each frame individually as you would work on single blocks in a traditional quilt and then add the black film borders around the edges, like sashing around blocks. In a way, this was similar to a sampler quilt. Every block was different, but they were designed to go together.

CREATING A PATTERN: For most of my pieced quilts, I create a pattern of some sort. In this case, I did not. I cut a piece of muslin larger than the quilt's finished size and then used a fabric marker to draw the 36" square outline on the muslin. I kept this on my design wall throughout construction, pinning frames in place and adjusting as necessary. I did not incorporate the muslin; it was simply a tool, later recycled into another project. When I needed specific dimensions for a block or for placement, I referred to the working sketch I had created to scale.

Tee Shirt Blocks

Four of the blocks are made with tee shirts from Michael's personal collection. Because tee shirts tend to stretch and sag, I had decisions to make. For the Bellagio tee shirt (top left), the Philadelphia Eagles tee shirt (bottom left), and the Penn's Landing blues event tee shirt (cat playing guitar), I fused woven stabilizer on the back of the tee shirt fabric before I cut and pieced it into the quilt. For the Preservation Hall tee shirt (center of the right edge), I didn't bother to back the knit fabric. The piece was so small, I simply quilted it enough to keep it in place. The red background is all fabric from a Rock and Roll Hall of Fame tee shirt.

Tuxedo Block

This block gave me heartburn! It wasn't a difficult block, but I had one tuxedo and only one chance to get it right. The block includes the tuxedo jacket, shirt, bowtie, studs, and pocket square.

I had two main challenges in constructing this block: Layering the shirt and jacket and cutting them to size while keeping the layers intact, and visually separating the black tuxedo from the black film frame.

First, I buttoned the shirt and put it on a hanger; then I added the jacket and buttoned it closed. To determine where the cutting lines would be, I created a window template by cutting a block-sized hole into a larger piece of paper and moved it around until I was happy with the view. I wanted to include both lapels and the breast pocket. I marked the cutting line with tailor's chalk.

With a long needle and contrasting thread, I hand-basted the layers together (shirt and jacket fronts) just inside what would be the stitching line. I planned to remove the basting after the block was constructed and attached to the film sashing. I slid a cutting mat inside the shirt and used my rotary cutter and ruler to cut out the block. I handled the layers as little as possible to avoid shifting. There was

Tee shirt block.

Tuxedo block.

probably a better way to cut this block, but I decided to implement an important lesson I have learned. Sometimes it's better to use a method that you're confident will work than to spin your wheels looking for the perfect way to do something.

Before I attached the film sashing, I needed to find a way to visually separate the black tuxedo from the black frame. Using one of Michael's long silk ties, I created a tiny piping and stitched it inside the seam connecting the tuxedo block to the sashing.

Hawaiian Shirt Blocks

I used two Hawaiian shirts in this quilt: both are in the upper right part of the quilt, above and below the sashing with the words "Goodnight, Sweetheart." The shirt fabrics were not stable; one was silk and the other was a loosely woven blend. To keep them stable, I used foundation fabric. I did not fuse them, but I used some strategically placed stitching to keep the layers together. During the quilting phase, I anchored these shirts further.

Unique Blocks

Two of the blocks came from unexpected sources.

The tan block in the lower right corner is made from a dress shirt. What I needed here was a plain background fabric to showcase the QuiltWriting and artifacts. I added the suspender first by stitching along both edges and then basting the top and bottom so they would be caught in the sashing seams. The QuiltWriting was added as part of the quilting phase and the Marilyn Monroe watch was added after all quilting was completed.

The woven block at the center bottom is made from a sock. Since the block was so small, I looked for a pattern that would look good but not distract from the other blocks. In a quilt this small, every choice is important. Michael loved his socks.

CREATING THE FILM EFFECT: I puzzled over how to create the illusion of sprocket holes in the "film" without actually creating holes. I could have used appliqué or reverse appliqué, but that seemed like a lot of work for very little return. The sprocket holes were not the stars of this quilt. I just needed to create the illusion and move on to more important aspects of the quilt.

There's a lesson here. If you have limited time or patience, decide where the bulk of your time should be spent and then try to figure a way to streamline some of the other parts of the project.

Using the sketch I made to scale, I figured out how many inches I would need for the edges of the film. Then, I used blue painter's tape to mask the black fabric, leaving only the sprocket holes showing. The tape looked like a ladder with two long sides and lots of crossbars. Once the tape was burnished in place, I painted the holes with iridescent black Paintstiks® and a stencil brush. This method was fast, easy, and fun.

Hawaiian shirt blocks.

Unique blocks.

45

QuiltWriting.

QUILTING, QUILTWRITING, AND ARTIFACTS: I think quilters are also part engineer. To complete this quilt, I had to add quilting, QuiltWriting, and the artifacts. The engineering challenge was to decide what came first. For this quilt, the order was quilting, QuiltWriting, and then artifacts.

QUILTING: Most of the quilting was stitch in the ditch work. I like ditchwork because it defines straight lines and keeps them crisp. It also allows structural quilting, quilting that holds the layers together without the distraction of visible stitching.

I started by quilting in the ditch along each side of the film and then around the sprocket holes to define them further and make them look more like appliqué. I also outlined each block.

For the tuxedo block, I quilted under the lapels to keep the jacket shape looking crisp, and I used free motion quilting for the Penn's Landing blues event block (cat playing electric guitar), allowing the flames and the cat shape to dictate the quilting lines.

For the floral Hawaiian shirt, I machine quilted along the front edge next to the buttons, and I hand quilted around a few of the flowers. I chose to hand quilt on the silk Hawaiian shirt because I didn't want to overwhelm the shirt with quilting, but I had to keep the lightweight silk firmly attached to the other layers of the quilt.

QUILTWRITING: This quilt contains examples of QuiltWriting in various sizes and configurations. For more information about QuiltWriting, see **page 57**.

I quilted the headlines ("Too Much Soul to Control," "The Maven," and "Goodnight, Sweetheart") in a 28-weight (quilting weight) thread to make the taller letters stand out. A thinner thread would have made skinnier letters. I also used 50-weight (piecing weight) thread to QuiltWrite the smaller text (on the green and white ribbon above and below the suspender and to the right of the suspender).

ARTIFACTS: Deciding when to attach the artifacts takes some planning. You need to consider the piecing and quilting that will surround the item you are attaching.

The Philadelphia Restaurant School graduation medal on the green and white ribbon (upper right corner) was attached after all of the piecing and quilting were completed. I stitched along the edges of the ribbon, completed the QuiltWriting on the ribbon, and then used gold thread to anchor the medal in place.

The suspender, in the lower right corner, was attached during the piecing process because I needed to catch the ends in the sashing. The watch face went on after the piecing, quilting, and QuiltWriting were completed, and the small book and reading glasses went into the Hawaiian shirt pocket last. My client and I talked about that book and how permanently I should attach it to the quilt. In the end, we decided to secure it with Velcro® dots to keep it in place, but still allow her access to take it out from time to time. The reading glasses are fastened at the upper hinge with a few stitches.

PERSONALIZING THE LABEL: This quilt has four labels — a general quilt label that contains the quilt's name, my information, why this quilt was made, and a sepia tone portrait of Michael and his wife; a label with things that didn't fit on the front of the quilt that my client wanted to include, such as the Hopi Prayer and a quote from the many e-mails she received after Michael died; and two Show Labels, which I added to document that this quilt appeared in two quilt shows.

NAMING THE QUILT: When I asked my client how she came up with the title for the quilt, she told me a heartwarming story about Michael's memorial service. One of the speakers, a dear friend of Michael's, held up a fictitious cookbook with a custom dust jacket that he had created for his presentation. He asked the attendees if they knew that Michael had been writing a cookbook. People looked around both confused and amused because they didn't know about any such cookbook, but the story was believable. The speaker went on to give the cookbook's title: "Too Much Soul to Control." There was more to the story, but the title stuck. Michael did, in fact, have too much soul to control.

The Quilt's Future

Making this quilt made me wish I had known Michael. Throughout the process, I feel like I got to know him. I listened to the playlist of songs from his memorial service CD while I worked: Bruce Springsteen, the Doors, the Kinks, Frank Sinatra, Clifton Chenier — they all kept me focused on the energy and vitality I wanted to infuse into the quilt.

The quilt will remain in Mrs. Kaye's private collection indefinitely. However, at some future point in time, the quilt may be donated to the Leukemia and Lymphoma Society as a permanent tribute to all those who have died, as Michael did, from this deadly blood cancer.

Labels from the back of *Too Much Soul to Control* by Cyndi Souder. *Courtesy of Linda Lee Kaye.*

Celebration Quilt Toolbox

I believe all quilters, no matter their experience, have quilting toolboxes. These toolboxes contain the skills, experiences, and knowledge we have acquired over our lifetimes. Notice that I didn't say "over our quilting lifetimes." Your quilting toolbox is filled with these quilt-related lessons:

• What you've learned in quilting classes and from DVDs
• What you've read in quilting books and magazines
• What you've experienced while making quilts on your own
• What you've absorbed while making quilts with groups

Your quilting toolbox also contains these experiences that are not directly related to quilting:

• Any hand and machine sewing you've done
• Any crafts you have done
• Any experience with color, including choosing paint colors or arranging flowers
• Any art training you have had, including fingerpainting in kindergarten
• Any puzzles you have completed or problems you have solved

All of your experiences, quilting or not, are in your quilting toolbox, waiting for you to take them out and use them.

In this section of the book, I've included some basic resources and some techniques I recommend. I think these additions to your toolbox are particularly important for Celebration Quilts, but they can certainly be used for any quilts in your future.

Knits

Because they are knit, tee shirts pose a special challenge in quilts. Knit fabrics stretch and sag, creating an uneven surface. If that's the effect you want, then you've added a tool to your quilting toolbox. If, however, you want the tee shirt to stay flat and smooth on your quilt, you'll need to stabilize the knit fabric. The key here is to fuse the tee shirt to something stable like woven interfacing before you cut the piece you want to use. Otherwise, the knit could curl and distort. If you are piecing with knit fabric, I recommend foundation piecing on woven fabric to add stability.

Silks

Silk offers two special challenges: it frays and it's often slippery.

To combat fraying:
- If your silk is washable, I recommend prewashing it before cutting and sewing. Washing can compress the fibers and tighten the weave. This will not work with all silk.

- Handle the silk as little as possible. Try not to move cut pieces from place to place. If you must relocate your cut pieces, place them on a small cutting mat that you can move. Minimize contact with the cut edges.

- Sew an edge finish on the cut edges. If you draw your seam line, then you can finish your edges before you sew your seams. If you are relying on your 1/4" foot to ensure a consistent seam allowance, then finish the edges after your seams are sewn.

- Draw your seam line and then serge your seams.

- As last resort, I'll use a liquid fray-stopping product. This sometimes stiffens or discolors the silk, so test first on a scrap.

When I think of quilts, I think of cotton. With Celebration Quilts, however, other fabrics are often in the mix. Tee shirts, silk ties, and wedding dresses can create challenges when it's time to piece and quilt intricate designs. In this section, I share some tips for handling difficult fabrics.

Detail of *Racing* begun by Pat Vincentz and finished by Linda Cooper. Tee shirt quilt. *Courtesy of Pat and Chet Vincentz.*

Picking Up the Pieces: Tragedy by Cyndi Souder. Depicts the horror of the September 11, 2001 events. The black netting symbolizes the smoke.

To keep the layers from slipping out of place:

• Use lots and lots of very sharp, very thin pins. Position them perpendicular to the edge of your fabric to make them easy to remove as you stitch.

• Hand baste your seams just inside the seam allowance. I wouldn't do this if I had a lot of seams, but I have done this when the project requires it, especially with curves.

Sheer Fabrics

Sheer fabrics come in many forms, including organza, organdy, tulle, netting, voile, and fabric simply called "sheer." These fabrics can be flat or crinkled; plain, printed, or embroidered; crisp or soft; simply colored or iridescent. With this wide array of choices, sheer fabrics provide quilters with lots of options.

Sheers and organza can be a challenge to work with because they tend to be slippery and they can easily stretch out of shape. To control them while you work, use the same techniques you would for silk *(see **page 49**).*

Sheers can be your secret weapon

• Is something too bright in your quilt? Cover it with a sheer.

• Is one of your colors a little off? Audition a sheer as a top layer. It might be just the thing to correct that color.

• Do you need to add dimension to a part of your quilt that looks flat and uninspired? Try stamping images or words on a sheer and then layering it on top of the uninspired section.

• Do you want to add texture without adding a lot of color? Try folding, tucking, or ruching sheers and adding that to the surface of your quilt. How about some sheer origami?

• Do you want to add a small artifact like a coin or seashell but there's no hole to use for sewing it into place? Sew a layer of sheer over the artifact and enclose it against the surface of your quilt or create a small bag or pouch. The item is now secure and you can still see it.

• Do you want to add an image? Print it with your inkjet printer on printer-ready ExtravOrganza®, following the manufacturer's directions.

Options for how to add sheer to your quilt

Sheers are often used as a top layer with a base fabric, but they can also be added to the completed quilt top.

- **LAYER IT WITH THE BASE FABRIC:** Add the sheer to the bottom layer before piecing and then treat the two layers together as if they were one fabric. You may want to use pins, basting, or spray adhesive to keep the layers together depending on size.

- **FUSE IT:** Fuse the sheer in place. I prefer Mistyfuse® for fusing in general, but I especially like it for fusing sheers. It doesn't show through, it doesn't add bulk, and it creates a reliable bond.

- **SEW IT:** Hand or machine stitch the sheer in place after the other piecing is done. You can leave the edges unfinished, you can fray them a little, or you can finish the edges before you stitch the sheer in place.

Stamping on sheers

Rubber stamping on sheer fabric is a great way to add visual texture and depth. I use fabric ink or any dye-based ink I have on hand. Remember to protect your work surface from the ink, which will stamp right through the open weave of the sheer fabric. Trust me; I've learned this the messy way!

Audition lots of fabrics when you are choosing the base fabric to use under your sheer layer. You'll be amazed at the different effects you can achieve with color and pattern.

Tsunami by Meghan J. Welch. The hands were created from sheer fabric. *Courtesy of the artist.*

Using Photographs

Using photographs in your Celebration Quilts infuses life into your work. Generally, you can add photos to your quilts by using phototransfer techniques, attaching the original photograph directly onto the face of your quilt, or printing them directly onto your fabric.

Phototransfer

Phototransfer techniques allow you to print your image on a variety of media and then transfer that image from the media to fabric. I've done this using transfer paper, transparency film, and even plain paper. Since I find printing on fabric is easier, I rarely use phototransfer techniques.

Using the Original Photograph

I've seen work where the original photograph was attached directly to the quilt. While I like the layered effect, I worry about the wear and tear the paper photograph will suffer. I would only use this method if the photo you are using is a duplicate and you won't mind if it is damaged by handling or sunlight.

Printing Directly onto Fabric

I prefer to print images directly onto my fabric. I use my inkjet printer and I usually print on purchased printer-ready fabric. When the quilt will benefit from a different look, I print directly onto my own fabric, backing it with freezer paper to stabilize it for the printer. By following the steps below, you will find that printing directly onto fabric is not as complicated as it seems.

1. **PREPARE THE IMAGE:** To print from your computer, you'll need a digital image. If you are using printed photographs, you'll need to scan them or use a digital camera to photograph the print.

   Before I print, I like to process the images in Photoshop Elements® by Adobe. You could use any photo-editing software, including the one that comes with your computer. I start by checking the color and correcting it if necessary. Some light sources add color casts that detract from the image, and you can easily correct that. Most photo-editing software also allows you to play with effects that will transform your image into old-fashioned sepia tones or change the colors completely for a Pop Art feel. You could also print your images in black and white and then add tints of color once the printing is heat set.

   Finally, I like to experiment with cropping the image. The look and feel of the image can be drastically altered by simply changing the boundaries of the photograph. Experiment until you're happy.

2. **PREPARE THE FABRIC:** Your fabric choices are only limited by what you can run through your printer. For portraits, I like to choose the smoothest fabric with the highest thread count to keep the weave of the fabric from being obvious in the subject's face. Also, smoother fabric will give you better print quality. For faces, I particularly like Electric Quilt's Cotton Lawn because the fabric is so smooth.

Detail of *50 Years of Marriage* by Cyndi Souder. *Courtesy of Signa and John Souder.*

Detail of *Voyages* by Kathy Lincoln. *Courtesy of the artist.*

Dad by Judy Vincentz Gula. *Courtesy of the artist.*

I like using purchased printer-ready fabric because I don't have to pre-treat it with chemicals or take the time to back it with freezer paper. Sometimes the quilt will benefit from printing on your own fabric. I've printed on batiks with great success. I have friends who pre-treat their fabric with Bubble Jet Set® and swear by the results. I don't pre-treat my fabric, although I do prewash it to remove any chemicals or sizing left over from the manufacturing process.

To run your own fabric through your printer, you'll need to back it for stability. I like to use freezer paper for this, but I'm told that fusible web is a good alternative. To use freezer paper, press the wrong side of your fabric to the waxy side of the freezer paper using a dry iron. Then trim the stabilized fabric to size. In my case, this is 8-1/2" x 11". I use a rotary cutter to get smoother edges. If there are any loose threads, cut them rather than pulling. At this point, I often press the cut edges lightly to confirm a good tight bond. Pay special attention to the corners. To secure the edge that will enter the printer first, you could run a piece of blue painter's tape like binding along the edge.

3. **PREPARE THE PRINTER:** You can print on any inkjet printer, but it's best to use one that feeds from the back, minimizing the curling and rolling the fabric must do before it exits the printer. Do not use a laser printer. You will also get better results with pigment or Durabright ink. You can use a printer with dye-based ink, but the colors will not be as bright and will not be color- or light-fast.

   Adjust your printer settings before you print. All printers are slightly different; read your printer manual to see what will work best for you. I set the printer to photo, but not best photo. The best photo setting will lay down a lot of ink that will rinse out and be wasted or could run on your fabric. I also set the printer for plain or bright white paper.

4. **PRINT:** I always run a test print on paper. Always. Yes, you'll use some of your ink, but I'd rather waste ink than the fabric.

   Once I'm happy with the test on paper, I print on my fabric. I hover over the printer as the fabric feeds in, and I hover in front of my printer as the printed fabric comes out. I never walk away when the fabric is printing. I'd rather be nearby if there's a jam or malfunction. Do not pull or "help" the fabric exit the printer. Any interference can cause irregularities in your printing and you'll need to print again.

5. **AFTER PRINTING:** If I've used printer-ready fabric, I read and follow the manufacturer's directions for dry time and rinsing. If I've used my own fabric, I set it aside and give it at least thirty minutes to dry. I then peel apart the freezer paper and the fabric and decide if I need to let it dry some more. Using a dry iron, I heat set the printed fabric between layers of paper towel and then I'm ready to use my fabric photographs.

Ideas for Using Your Fabric Photographs

I believe the real challenge comes once your photograph is on fabric. How do you add photographs to your quilt without making the quilt look like fabric with a bunch of random photos on it?

• **SCRAPBOOK PAGE** — If you want your quilt to look like a scrapbook page, then go for it! Embrace the concept fully and add elements to enhance the effect. Consider making tiny black or gold corners for your photos like the adhesive ones we used to use back in the scrapbook dark ages. Think about including captions with names and dates, either printed or handwritten. Anything you would do in a paper scrapbook can be reproduced in fabric.

• **INTEGRATE THE FABRIC PHOTOS** — With some patterns, the printed photographs would fit nicely as a repeating element. Imagine a log cabin quilt with photographs in the center squares. This would also work nicely with friendship star, shoofly, or any block pattern built around a central square set straight or on point.

• **HIGHLIGHT THE FABRIC PHOTOS** — If you want the printed photographs to take center stage, then frame them with borders or sashing. Photographs in a grid layout with attic window sashing could be really effective. With the right fabric choices, the attic window pattern could give the illusion of depth.

• **CREATE ART WITH THE FABRIC PHOTOS** — What if you treated the printed photographs as regular fabric and fussy cut certain elements as you construct your design? If you are creating a family quilt, why not create a family tree and use the photographs to fussy cut leaves? Or choose an existing pattern that feels modern and use the photographs for certain recurring elements. BlueUndergroundStudios.com has some patterns that would be great candidates for this treatment.

• **CREATE A TIMELINE OR HISTORY WITH THE FABRIC PHOTOS** — Organize your printed photographs into a timeline or into family groups. This would help children get to know their relatives, especially those who live too far away to visit often. A quilt with family pictures could also be helpful for family members who are aging and could use the visual reminders of their history.

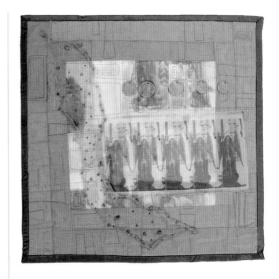

Joan of Arc by Judy Vincentz Gula. Photographs are printed on organza. *Courtesy of the artist.*

Detail of *Ed's Quilt* by Ellie Flaherty. *Courtesy of Edward J. Flaherty.*

I believe the magic happens during the quilting stage of the project, but it doesn't happen on its own. Effective quilting takes planning.

Stitch in the Ditch

When I begin the quilting stage of any project, I always start with any ditch work — stitching in the ditch — that needs to be done. There are two advantages to this approach:

1. The construction lines that you want to appear straight will maintain their precision. I also quilt in the ditch around some shapes to maintain their clear outlines.

2. The ditch work will anchor the layers of the quilt and allow you to take out some of the pins (or basting) holding the layers together. This is a nice preparation for stippling or any fancier quilting that you plan to do.

Stitch in the Ditch Tip:

Do you ever worry that your quilting in the ditch won't actually land right next to the seam? I like to use a magnifier in front of the needle — either a freestanding magnifier on a gooseneck stand or the smaller magnifiers that Bernina® offers for my machine. When you look through the magnifier, the ditch looks more like a canyon! Just keep it slow and you'll be able to stitch in the ditch every time.

Example of stitching in the ditch, sewn in contrasting thread for purposes of illustration.

QuiltWriting

I like to incorporate writing or text in my quilts. Sometimes I print directly on fabric using my printer, rubber stamp letters with paint or ink, or write directly on my quilt top with fabric pens. My favorite way to add writing is to stitch it in as part of the quilting stage. Over the years, I've developed a technique I call QuiltWriting, where I stitch the words in with free motion quilting.

The steps are simple: decide what you want to write, lay out the words, and free motion quilt them into your quilt.

STEP 1: DECIDE WHAT WORDS YOU WANT TO INCLUDE

Deciding what to write can be a challenge. It's better to have too much so that you can choose the best material. To get you started, here are a few ideas:

• Include words that have to do with the purpose of the quilt. This might mean birthday wishes, names of family members, memories from a wedding day, or words from your heart.

• Consider adding quotes. Are there words that you have shared with the quilt's intended recipient that would add meaning to your Celebration Quilt?

• Are there poems or song lyrics that would make this more meaningful? Be aware of copyright issues and use these words for personal use, not for sale. I like to give credit for someone else's writing if I can find the source.

Detail of *Too Much Soul to Control* by Cyndi Souder. *Courtesy of Linda Lee Kaye.*

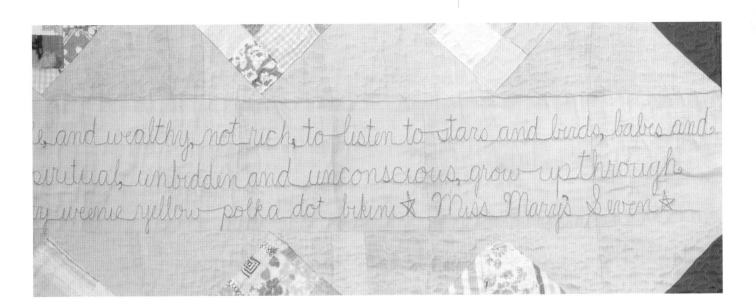

Detail of *Remembering Mary*, created by Mary W. Kerr and quilted by Cyndi Souder. *Courtesy of Mary W. Kerr.*

Step 2: Lay Out the Words

Depending on your comfort level, you may want to lay out the words before you quilt, or you may want to just get started with the stitching. If I'm working on client work or if the piece will really look off if I haven't planned the word spacing, then I lay everything out in advance. Here's how:

• If you've never tried to free motion quilt words, try it now. You'll need a sample to see how big you generally write. Try to make a sample with the same materials and thread you're using in your project. If you've tried QuiltWriting before, take out your sample now.

• Using your favorite word processing program, type in the words you want to add to your quilt. I use Microsoft Word for this step. Choose a font that looks like handwriting. I like Lucida Handwriting, since the letters are connected. Change your page layout to landscape and then increase the size of the font until the words are about the same size as the QuiltWriting on your sample. If you'd prefer, you could increase the font size until it's about right for the space you have on the quilt and then adjust the scale of your QuiltWriting accordingly. Either way will work.

• Print, cut the lines apart (above and below the writing), and tape the writing in order into strips.

• Now you can use these strips to lay out your words on your project.

• Either pin them directly where you want the QuiltWriting to go (great if you used thin paper that will easily come away after you perforate it by stitching through it) or pin the strips below where you want to QuiltWrite and use them as guides.

Step 3: Decide how to use the guide strips

When I teach this workshop, I offer three ways to use the strips you created in the last step: stitch directly through paper, use the printed strips as guides, or keep the strips nearby but QuiltWrite without them on the surface of your project.

• **Stitch directly through paper.** Stitching through paper is like QuiltWriting with training wheels! All you have to do is follow the lines. To do this, trace the printed guide onto thin paper like tracing paper or deli paper. I have a roll of medical exam room paper I use for this because I can make my strips as long as I like. Cut the new strips that you just traced and pin them onto the surface of your project just where you want the words to go. Free motion quilt directly through this paper, keeping your stitches short to perforate the paper along the stitching lines for easy paper removal.

• **Use the printed strips as guides.** If you'd rather not stitch through paper, you can place the guides above where you want the words to go and then refer to them as you work. The guides will give you the correct spacing, but you'll be able to see exactly where the words are going without the paper getting in the way. I pin the guides in place so that my words are laid out exactly as I want them.

• **Keep the guide strips nearby, but QuiltWrite without them.** Once you've seen how much writing will fit in the space and you have a feel for the size of the writing, then you may not need to have the guides directly in front of you. You may be able to set them aside and QuiltWrite without the distraction of paper in your way. Be brave; try it!

Step 4: Time to QuiltWrite!

If you've never tried to write using free motion quilting, don't worry — it's easier than you think! Before you start, I have a few tips and tricks to help ensure your success.

• Set your sewing machine up for free motion quilting: feed dogs down, free motion quilting foot on, thread tension adjusted using a test quilt sandwich made of the same materials as your project. I like to use gloves to give me more traction when I'm quilting.

• Your top thread color should contrast with the quilt top. Otherwise, you may not see the words! Also consider using a thicker thread to increase the visibility of all your fancy work.

• If you're having any thread pop (bobbin thread pulled to the top and showing in little dots) and you cannot adjust this satisfactorily by loosening the top thread tension, then use the same color

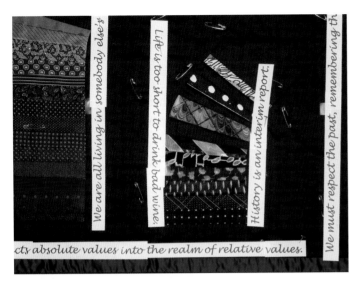

Detail of *Mentor, Guru and Sage* quilt top with printed strips used to lay out QuiltWriting.

Detail of *Mentor, Guru and Sage* quilt top with printed strip laid out in preparation for QuiltWriting above the strip.

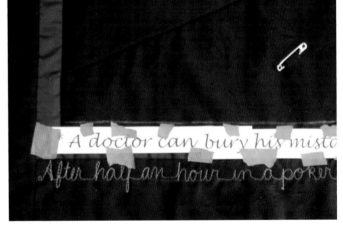

Detail of *Mentor, Guru and Sage* quilt top with printed strip laid out in preparation for QuiltWriting above the strip.

Detail of *Mentor, Guru and Sage* quilt top with the first line of QuiltWriting done.

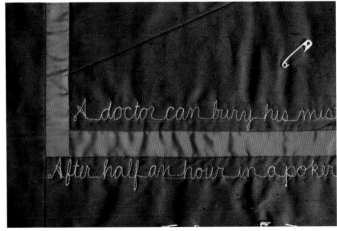

Detail of *Mentor, Guru and Sage* quilt top with second line of QuiltWriting done.

thread in the bobbin as for the top. If the top thread is variegated, then try to match the tone of the color. Don't waste the variegated thread in the bobbin unless you like the look for the back; there's no chance the color variations on top and bottom will line up when you're sewing.

• Keep all of your letters and words connected. Remember, every time you stop and start, you'll have more thread ends to bury when you're finished quilting. Leave extra space between words and cross every "t" on your way back down. Otherwise, you'll have to come back for it and you'll just create more ends to bury.

• If it's your first time to QuiltWrite, start by writing your name.

• Work in a calm environment. If your kids are running around the house, you may not be able to concentrate and you might have to rip out misspelled words. I'm speaking from experience. Take breaks to keep your head clear.

Special Designs

Sometimes there's a special design I want to include in the quilting. For *Mentor, Guru and Sage* (page 30), it was a cartoon that had been drawn to honor the subject of the Celebration Quilt. You could use this technique for any design from feather wreaths to portraits. Here's how I do it:

• Trace the design on very thin paper (tracing paper, deli paper, or exam room paper work well). Use a fine point that's about the same size as your thread so that you get an idea of how the design will look when it is stitched.

• Pin the design in place on the quilt sandwich.

• Using quilting or heavier-weight thread in a contrasting color, quilt right through the paper, following the lines.

• Remove the paper gently. The needle perforates the paper and most of it will tear easily to be removed. For the stubborn paper caught in tight places, use pointy tweezers.

Of course, you can always quilt your special designs freehand, but I like the insurance I get by using a pattern.

"Art Law" cartoon to be reproduced in quilting on *Mentor, Guru and Sage. Courtesy of Wendy Luke.*

Quilted cartoon on *Mentor, Guru and Sage* by Cyndi Souder. *Photograph by Thom Goertel. Courtesy of Wendy Luke.*

Step 1: Cut the Fabric.

From a sturdy woven fabric, cut a strip 10" wide by one inch less than the width of your finished quilt. If your quilt is 18" wide, you would cut a 10" x 17" strip of fabric.

Step 2: Finish the Ends

Hem the 10" ends of the unsewn sleeve by turning under 1/4" hem, pressing, turning under another 1/4" hem, and pressing again. Then, stitch in place. This covers the raw edges and creates a strong end for the sleeve. In case you care about thread color, this is the stitching that will show on your sleeve. Choose your thread accordingly. I've used contrasting thread on the sample sleeve to highlight the construction.

Hem the 10" ends.

Step 3: Construct the Tube

Fold the strip WRONG sides together so that the hems are at each end and the tube is now 5" wide. I press at this stage to make things easier. Stitch along the raw edge side, taking a 1/2" seam allowance, and then BASTE along the fold 1/2" from the edge. Yes, it sounds weird, but it's important to do this.

Stitch regularly along one side and baste along the other side a half-inch from the edge.

Hanging Sleeves

I think it's important to have a well-made, fully functional hanging sleeve on your quilt if you ever plan to hang your work. Many quilt shows require a 4" sleeve and some will send your quilt back if the sleeve is too small for the poles they use to hang the show. Hanging sleeves are easy to make and go together quickly.

Back of *Faith and Love* by Cyndi Souder.
Courtesy of Suzanne Souder and Glenn Rill.

Hanging Sleeve Tips

Making a hanging sleeve shouldn't feel like drudgery. Look at it as another way to personalize the quilt; attach the sleeve to the quilt while you are sewing on your quilt label. You can save time by doing all of the hand sewing at one time.

- *To make your sleeve less noticeable, use the same fabric you used for the quilt back.*

- *To make a statement with your sleeve, use a high contrast fabric or a fabric that says something about the quilt. For Faith and Love, I made the sleeve from fabric that came out in the year 2000 to commemorate the year the wedding took place.*

- *If you're worried that your quilt will not hang flat, make an extra sleeve for the bottom of the quilt and put a wood or metal slat into the bottom sleeve for weight.*

STEP 4: FINISH THE SLEEVE

Press the sleeve so that the seam (raw edges) and the basting (folded edge) are nested together, one on top and one against the ironing board. I flip the seam allowance in one direction and the folded edge in the other direction. The task becomes a bit more challenging for longer sleeves.

Press the tube so that the two seams (one basted and the other one sewn) nest together.

Pin the sleeve to the quilt with the raw edge seam underneath and the basted seam on top.

STEP 5: ATTACH THE SLEEVE TO THE QUILT BACK

Pin the sleeve to the back of your quilt, centered left to right, with the top of the sleeve about 1" below the top of the quilt. The raw edges should be against the quilt and the basted fold should be away from the quilt. Do not take the shortcut of stitching the sleeve into the binding. Yes, it will save you time, but you run the risk of seeing the top of the sleeve from the front once the quilt is hung.

Now, hand-stitch around all four sides of the sleeve, including the ends where the sleeve is open. If you don't, the people who hang your quilt are likely to slip the pole between the sleeve and your quilt instead of *inside* the sleeve, leaving potential yucky residue on your artwork. When you stitch, try to catch the sleeve and the quilt backing only. If you go all the way through, your stitches will show on the front. If you catch too much batting, the quilt front could dimple a bit.

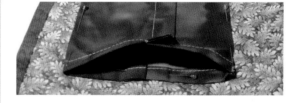

Be sure to sew the ends of the sleeve to the quilt.

STEP 6: FINISH THE SLEEVE

Now, rip out the basting that you stitched 1/2" away from the fold. This makes the outside of the sleeve a little longer than the side that's against the quilt back, creating ease to go around the pole. If you don't create this ease, the top of your quilt can appear rounded when the pole is in the sleeve. If you've seen this effect, you know why you want to avoid it.

Hand-stitch the sleeve to the back of the quilt, with the top of the sleeve about 1" from the top of the quilt.

Label Contents

In general, quilt labels have a single purpose: documentation. At a bare minimum, quilt labels should have these elements:

- **Quilter's Name:** As much as we'd like to think of ourselves as unique, a quick Google search will show that most of us share our names with others. Consider including some sort of identifier in addition to your name: city and state, maiden name, or website would all be good additions to your name. Make it easy for future quilt historians to trace your work.

- **Date:** Include either the date you completed the quilt or the date you gave the quilt away. If there's a story behind the dates, include that. I have one quilt that took me seven years to complete. I didn't include that on the label, but I probably should have.

I'd like you to consider other things you might want to add to your quilt label from now on. You may not want to include all of these items on every label, but keep them in mind as options. Think about who will own the quilt and what they might like to see on the label.

- **Quilt name:** Do you want to go through your life referring to one of your quilts as "that quilt with the tee shirts and the fish fabric?" No? Then give it a name — and put the name on the label. If you have trouble coming up with a name, take the quilt to a bee or guild meeting. Your friends will have plenty of opinions.

- **The occasion for which you made the quilt:** If you made this quilt for a special occasion, include that on your label. For a wedding, you would probably include the couple's names and their wedding date. Baby quilts are often presented before the baby's birth; we often need to add the label after the birth so that we have the baby's name and the correct date.

- **The story behind the quilt:** Why did you make this quilt? Was it a gift? A challenge? If you participated in a challenge, it's a good idea to include the name of the challenge and any other information you have about the challenge, including the rules, the host, and how you came up with your idea based on the challenge guidelines.

- **Names of everyone who worked on the quilt:** If this was a group quilt, include the names of all of the quilters who contributed work or materials. If the quilt was quilted by a longarm or hand quilter, include their name as well. If you can get signatures, that adds meaning to the label. If not, then print the names.

- **Pictures:** Are there pictures that would help tell the quilt's story? Add them to the label or print them separately and stitch or fuse them onto the back of the quilt. Are there pictures that would make the quilt more meaningful? If you're

I cringe whenever I hear quilters say they don't need to label their quilts. Your label will speak for you when you are not there with the quilt. It will tell the story of who you are and why you made the quilt. If you are celebrating an event or a person's life, the label will tell that as well.

Label from *49 Forever!* by Kathy Lincoln. Notice the signatures of friends who contributed blocks to celebrate this milestone birthday (not 49!). *Courtesy of the artist.*

Labels from *Too Much Soul to Control* by Cyndi Souder. Additional labels tell where the quilt has been and share material that wouldn't fit on the front. *Courtesy of Linda Lee Kaye.*

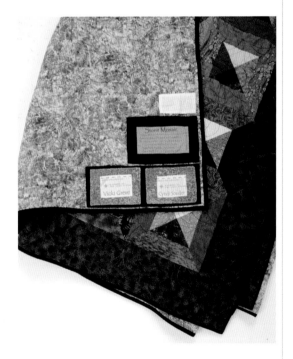

Labels from *Stone Mosaic* by Vicki Zacheis Greve and Cyndi Zacheis Souder, longarm quilted by Kathryn Gray, The Finishing Touch. This very large quilt includes quilt retreat blocks from both sisters and their retreat name tags.

making a baby quilt for a family member, think about including a picture of yourself on the label. If your Celebration Quilt commemorates someone who has passed, consider adding a picture of your lost loved one.

- **ANYTHING THAT WOULDN'T FIT ON FRONT OF THE QUILT:** Did you run out of room on the front of your quilt? Were there things you wanted to include but couldn't because they didn't look right? Did you have leftover blocks? Or did you have blocks from other quilters that arrived too late for you to include in the quilt top? Sew or fuse them to the back. If you included quotes or sayings on the front of the quilt, did you have leftovers? Print them on a label and include it on the back.

- **CARE INSTRUCTIONS:** If your quilt can be laundered, the recipients would probably appreciate instructions that include water temperature and dryer guidelines. If your quilt cannot be laundered, you owe it to the recipient to warn them so they do not ruin the quilt. If you make or give away numerous quilts that require the same care, print multiple care labels at one time and have them ready.

Creating the Label

I like to customize each label to suit the quilt. Generally, I think of labels in three categories: computer-generated, hand-lettered, and embroidered.

COMPUTER-GENERATED LABELS: I usually print the label using printer-ready fabric and my inkjet printer. Whatever brand of printer-ready fabric I use, I always follow the manufacturer's directions. If the package says to rinse the fabric after printing, I do that. After rinsing, resist the urge to wring out the label; those wrinkles will never go away. To make sure the rinsed labels are completely dry, I sandwich the printed sheet between layers of paper towel and press with a dry iron, which also heat-sets the ink.

PRINTING MY LABELS GIVES ME OPTIONS:

- I can match the font to the quilt. Computers come loaded with fonts and this is one place you can feel comfortable playing with them. Just make sure the finished label is easy to read.

- I can choose the font size. I might make the quilt name bigger than the rest of the information.

- I don't have to come up with original labels each time I print. I save all of my labels in one electronic folder. When it's time to create a new label, I open a file that's close to what I want and then I edit the information for the current quilt. This saves a lot of time and gives me a record of the quilts I've labeled.

- I can print images with the information on the label or on a separate label.

- Depending on the size of the labels, I can print more than one label on one sheet of fabric.

- I like printing on my own fabric. That way I can match the label fabric to one of the light colors from the front of the quilt.

HAND-LETTERED LABELS: If the quilt was pieced and quilted by hand or if the quilt celebrates handwork of some kind, then I make the label by hand.

If you're creating your label by hand, there are tools and techniques you can use to make the process quick and easy.

- Use a pen meant for fabrics. I prefer Pigma pens by Sakura. I do heat set the ink once I'm finished writing.

- To keep your writing straight, create a template of straight lines with the length and spacing you want and place it under your fabric. If you can't see it clearly through the fabric, place the template and fabric on a light box.

- Trace. Print what you want to say in a clear, easy-to-read font on a piece of paper. Adjust the font size if necessary. Now place the printed paper underneath your fabric and trace the words using a fabric marker. If you can't see the template clearly through your fabric, use a light box.

- While you're writing on your fabric, you may want to add some flourishes, flowers, or a frame. You could draw (or trace) these artistic touches in one color and then embellish them with other colors. Depending on how your quilt will be used and cared for, you could even add beads. That would be a nice touch for a wedding quilt.

- Writing or drawing on your fabric is easier if you can keep it flat and stationary. I use a Grip-n-Grip No-Slip Mat to keep the fabric from shifting. You could also press your fabric to the waxy side of some freezer paper or lay it on fine grit sandpaper.

EMBROIDERED LABELS: If you have the time and tools, you can embroider your quilt labels.

- Most sewing machines have built-in alphabets.

- Many embroidery machines come with basic software that allows you to create your own message.

- Most embroidery software will allow you to combine your words with other designs to create a truly special label.

- Embroidering the label will increase your fabric choices. You are only limited by your available thread colors and the types of fabric your machine will handle.

- You could also embroider your label by hand.

Label from *Power Suited Him* by Cyndi Souder. This label from my Power Suits Art Quilt Challenge entry includes my artist's statement as well as the original image from which the quilt and the challenge logo were developed.

Label from *Racing* begun by Pat Vincentz and finished by Linda Cooper. This is a neatly done example of printing the label text on paper and tracing it onto the label with a fabric marker. *Courtesy of Pat and Chet Vincentz.*

Make Your Own Light Box:

You don't need a light box to be able to trace onto your fabric. I create the same effect as a light box by placing my Sew Steady® Table over an open OttLite® lamp. If you have a sewing cabinet with a Plexiglas® insert, you could fashion that into a light table by placing a lamp below the insert. Just place your template and fabric on the Plexiglas and trace to your heart's content.

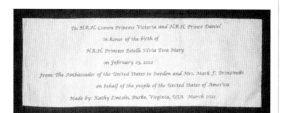

Label from *Royal Crowns* by Kathy Lincoln. The text was machine embroidered. *Courtesy of the artist.*

Label from *Batik Bear's Paw* by Cyndi Souder, longarm quilted by Kathryn Gray, The Finishing Touch. Leftover blocks from the quilt top create a special border for the label.

Multiple Labels:

If you're concerned about putting too much information on one label, consider using more than one label on your quilt. You could use one label for your information, one label for the story behind the quilt, and one label for care instructions. Or are you thinking that your existing quilts could benefit from additional documentation? Go for it! It's never too late to add more information.

Attaching the Label

Once the label is done, you need to attach it to the back of your quilt.

• **Placement:** Generally, I sew my labels on the lower right corner of the quilt back. Some quilters prefer to center their labels along the bottom of the quilt back. One savvy quilter I know centers her label along the bottom of the quilt but sews the label on upside-down! Then the label is right side up when you grasp the bottom of the quilt and roll it up from the bottom. Very clever!

• **Sew or Fuse?** I sew my labels on. It's just part of the handwork required to get my quilts done and I like how it looks. You could fuse your labels in place. That would certainly be faster and harder to remove in case your quilt falls into unscrupulous hands.

• **Label Security:** For quilts that will travel a lot, it's important to make sure the label stays on the quilt. I know a quilter who adds the label to the back before the quilt is layered and then she quilts through the label as part of the quilting process.

• **Label Borders:** I like to add borders to my labels. It makes them look more finished and the fabric I use for the label borders is usually easier to hand sew than the printer-ready fabric I use.

• **Leftover Blocks:** If I have any leftover blocks or pieced elements from the quilt top, I like to use them to enhance the label.

Special Label Treatment

Sometimes special quilts require special treatment for the label. These include the following:

• **Double-Sided Quilts:** If a quilt is designed with two fronts and no back, where do you put the label? When I created a double-sided quilt to commemorate the events of September 11, 2001, I gave no thought to the label. Once the quilt was finished, I realized the challenge would be hiding the label but keeping it accessible. The solution was to create a cover for the label that would blend into the quilt.

• **Fundraiser Quilts:** Sometimes you don't know where your quilt will land. When we created *Teal Beauty*, a quilt that was auctioned at a fundraiser for cancer research, I could not imagine that the new owners would want to see all of the label information each time they used the quilt. The solution was to construct a label that would open to show the quilt's documentation and close to discreetly hide the written information. For details on how this label was crafted, see the *Teal Beauty* section starting on page 20.

• **Where Have Your Quilts Been:** My local guild encloses labels when they return each quilt after the show. One of my labels says, "This quilt was exhibited at the 33rd Annual Quilters Unlimited Quilt Show, June 2-4, 2006." Whenever one of my quilts travels to a show, I try to make a special label to put on that quilt. I like the idea of documenting where my quilts have been.

Label from *Picking Up the Pieces* by Cyndi Souder. Because this quilt is double-sided, it was necessary to "hide" the label. In these images, the label is closed (top) and open (bottom).

Label from *Teal Beauty* by Cyndi Souder. The label is open. In the accompanying image, it is closed. *Courtesy of Nancy and Neil Weidner.*

Labels from *With This Ring* by Cyndi Souder. This quilt has labels for the couple edged with rubber stamped leaves and the one my guild show included when they returned the quilt to me. *Courtesy of Andrew Gay and Amy Rigney-Gay.*

Celebration Quilts Gallery

I love looking at quilts! Whenever I look at quilts, I learn things, I see things I've never seen before, and I'm energized to go make more quilts of my own. I especially love seeing Celebration Quilts. I'm fascinated by the many ways in which quilters share their feelings through their art. In this gallery of Celebration Quilts, I hope you learn things, see things you've never seen before, and are inspired and energized to go make your own Celebration Quilts.

There's something inherently optimistic about baby quilts. They are fresh, happy, and filled with positive energy. Often, baby quilts are done with quick piecing techniques; sometimes quilters make the same pattern over and over again, changing the fabric for each new quilt.

Baby Quilts

Liam's Baby Quilt by Cyndi Souder. While I normally avoid black as a dominant color for baby quilts, this quilt cried for it. Liam's room was painted a cheerful sunflower yellow and I had the benefit of a paint chip to use while shopping for fabric. Liam's parents are design-oriented and welcomed the bold baby quilt into the nursery. *Courtesy of Sean, Jenny, and Liam Sullivan.*

Thank You for the Music by Carol S. Fray, Libby Fritsche, Kathy Lincoln, Shanna Obelenus, Heidi Schwartz, Linda Snow, and Cyndi Souder. At a quilt retreat, my roommates and I listened to the wedding playlist from friends of mine who married in 2001. Later, when we learned they were expecting their first child, our small group made the happy couple a baby quilt. The pattern is "Lucky Stars" from Diane Atkinson. *Courtesy of Trevor Gay.*

Star Baby Quilt by Cyndi Souder. This is one of the first baby quilts I made. I drew the stars and paper-pieced them. This quilt was a gift to one of my husband's close friends for his first child. For this quilt, the soft batik fabrics drove the design. *Courtesy of David and Cindy Tikiob.*

Royal Crowns by Kathy Lincoln. Kathy was selected to create a baby quilt for the United States Ambassador to Sweden to present to the Crown Princess Victoria to celebrate the birth of Princess Estelle Silvia Ewa Mary. Kathy was asked to use red, white, and blue; other design decisions were left to her discretion. This pattern, "turnstile," is a traditional block. *Courtesy of the artist.*

Kathryn's Baby Quilt by Cyndi Souder. Knowing that my niece liked Beatrix Potter, I collected Beatrix Potter fabric when it came on the market and made this quilt for her daughter Kathryn. This quilt was designed to highlight the fabric, with fussy cut star centers and borders. The pattern is "Lucky Stars" from Diane Atkinson. *Courtesy of Kathryn Young.*

Simone's Baby Quilt by Cyndi Souder. I created this baby quilt for my sister and niece to present to a special friend for her first child. The pattern is the traditional puss in the corner block. *Courtesy of Ann-Marie Anderson.*

Weddings and Anniversaries

Weddings and anniversaries are special occasions. I love seeing quilts that mark these milestones. Often these quilts are signature quilts. They always seem intensely personal.

Faith and Love by Cyndi Souder. I made this quilt for my sister-in-law and her husband to celebrate their marriage. The center panel is a rubbing that I made from a headstone in the cemetery surrounding their church. I bordered it with the mossiest fabric I could find and then added some Celtic appliqué. *Courtesy of Suzanne Souder and Glenn Rill.*

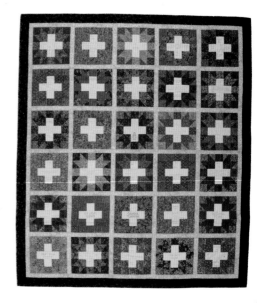

Joe's Tie Quilt by Linda Cooper. Linda made this quilt in memory of her father, Joseph A. Thoma, Jr., for his dear wife Edith. Joe and Edith were married for fifteen happy years before he died. While this is a tribute quilt for a lost loved one, it's also a celebration of marriage. The blue Ultrasuede® is from Edith's wedding suit; the brown is from Joe's suit; and, of course, the ties were his. Edith says if her house were burning, she'd save this quilt. *Courtesy of Edith Thoma.*

50th Anniversary Quilt by Shannon Shirley. This Celebration Quilt is made of signature blocks, which Shannon presented to her in-laws on their 50th anniversary. The quilt was finished shortly thereafter. The block is Greek cross. *Courtesy of the artist.*

50 Years of Marriage by Cyndi Souder. When my in-laws marked fifty years of marriage, the three kids threw them a party. I sent out signature blocks to all attendees and then made a quilt from the results using an attic window setting. If you do this, be sure to give complete instructions, including a line marking the quarter-inch seam allowance so that all writing will still be visible once the blocks are sewn. *Courtesy of Signa and John Souder.*

Celebration Quilts are sometimes made to pay tribute to our lost loved ones. These quilts can be particularly difficult to make because the subject matter is so raw and emotional. The process of making these quilts can be cathartic.

Voyages by Kathy Lincoln. Kathy made this quilt to commemorate the 20th anniversary of her grandparent's death. The pictures from 1905 through 1984 cover childhood, college graduation, passports, and their eight circumnavigations of the world. Kathy used silks, batiks, and cottons; she also printed photographs directly onto her fabric. She used the storm at sea block for structure. *Courtesy of the artist.*

Remembrance by Mary Ellen Hardin Simmons. Mary Ellen created this quilt to show how her family celebrates Armistice Day (now Veteran's Day) — by placing flags on the graves of veterans from her family who have died. This image shows her young granddaughter walking down the path toward a family grave. *Courtesy of the artist.*

Kay's Yellow Stars by Mary W. Kerr. Mary created this quilt for her Grandma Kay, using fabrics from Kay's collection of feed sacks, old clothes, and curtain fabric. This is a simple but effective way to showcase a fabric collection with a neutral background. *Courtesy of the artist.*

A Quilt for Connie Graham by Lesly-Claire Greenberg and Cookie Shuffleton, longarm quilted by Kathryn Gray, The Finishing Touch. Patsy Graham was a swimmer, a coach, a student at James Madison University, and a victim of bone cancer. Through the annual Patsy Graham Splash About invitational swim meet, money is raised to endow a scholarship at JMU in Patsy's name. Fundraiser tee shirts were designed by Lesly-Claire Greenberg. *Courtesy of Connie Graham.*

Remembering Annie by Jeanne Creekmore. Jeanne made this quilt to honor her aunt, Eunice Bonow Bardell. "Annie," as the children called her, was a registered pharmacist and an excellent seamstress who made all of her own clothes. The quilt is made from Annie's mementos including a dress, a pillowcase border, needlecrafts, and her pharmacist's badge. *Courtesy of the artist.*

I appreciate quilts that celebrate both past and current family traditions. Photographs are popular on these quilts, as are treasured artifacts.

The Thoma Jewels by Linda Cooper. Linda made this Celebration Quilt for her father, Joseph Thoma, who was the fourth generation to run the family jewelry store. The quilt has images of ancestors as well as the artist's brothers and nephew, adding the fifth and sixth generations to the dynasty. The 3-D log cabin settings represent different jewels. *Courtesy of Edith Thoma.*

Dad by Judy Vincentz Gula. This small quilt, created by Judy Vincentz Gula to honor her father, is packed with tradition. The photograph of the artist's father was phototransferred onto a hanky that belonged to his mother. The stylized monogram — initials he shared with his father — was taken from his father's handkerchief. It's wonderful when treasured artifacts work this well together. *Courtesy of the artist.*

Papa's 80 by Lisa Brehm Ellis. In this simple but effective quilt, Lisa celebrates her father's 80th birthday. Starting with an image printed on fabric, she added simple borders with some traditional half-square piecing detail and included some QuiltWriting in her quilting design. *Courtesy of the artist.*

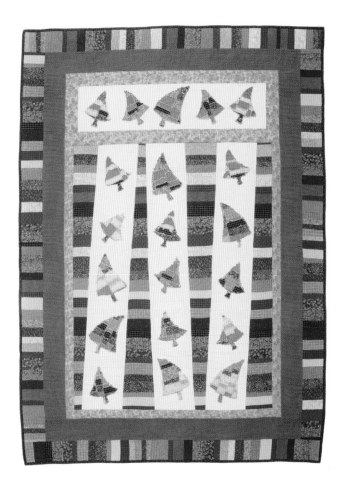

Ed's Quilt by Ellie Flaherty. Ellie Flaherty created this memory quilt to celebrate her father-in-law's 90th birthday. She printed photographs of family members, arranged them into groups, and stitched them onto this quilt. She describes this quilt as a picture of one man's life. The quilt hung in Ed's house where he saw it everyday and his caretakers were reminded that he had a family that loved him. *Courtesy of Edward J. Flaherty.*

Swaying Pines by Jean Welch. This is Jean's first quilt, made to commemorate the first Christmas season during which her daughter Meghan was deployed. A gift for her daughter, the quilt is infused with warmth and the reminder of swaying pines in the snowy Adirondack Mountains. In short, home. The quilt includes some QuiltWriting and lots of soft flannel. *Courtesy of Meghan J. Welch.*

Family by Judy Vincentz Gula. This quilt was created as a gift to the grandparents. Working with her son and the other grandchildren, Judy built this quilt around her mother's favorite color palette of red, white, and blue. The grandchildren made the handprints and helped sew the blocks. The artifacts come from the grandparents and Judy's collection of ephemera. Notice the pocket Judy used to attach the fan. *Courtesy of Pat and Chet Vincentz.*

Accomplishments

For merit awards, completed service, graduation, and other achievements, I like to celebrate with quilts. Remember to include the details on your label!

Eagle Scout for Ryan by Lisa Brehm Ellis. Lisa presented this quilt to her son, Ryan, at his Boy Scout Court of Honor when he attained the rank of Eagle Scout. *Courtesy of the artist.*

Racing by Pat Vincentz and Linda Cooper. This tee shirt quilt commemorates Chet Vincentz's involvement in the racing world as a driver and a supplier. His wife Pat started the quilt and asked Linda Cooper to assemble and complete it. The result is an effective and attractive setting for tee shirts. *Courtesy of Pat and Chet Vincentz.*

Friendship Chain President's Quilt by Susan Fernandez and Cyndi Souder with help from the Burke Chapter of Quilters Unlimited. Longarm quilted by Kathryn Gray, The Finishing Touch. This quilt was a group effort. I designed the friendship chain pattern to honor Susan for her hard work as our local guild president. I handed out instructions to the guild members and pieced the center panel from the resulting blocks. I also added the light border. Susan pieced the spectacular outer border and Kathy Gray quilted it. *Courtesy of Susan Fernandez.*

Ryan's Graduation Quilt by Mary W. Kerr. With the addition of some fused characters and a fireman's hat, this vintage nine patch and snowball quilt became a contemporary graduation quilt. Mary then invited guests at her son's graduation party to add their signatures and well wishes with fabric pens. *Courtesy of the artist.*

Whether you work with travel photos, collect exotic fabrics, or are simply immortalizing a memory, quilts made to celebrate travel can capture your trip in fabric and allow you to return whenever you desire

Travel and Destinations

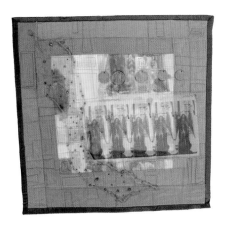

Joan of Arc by Judy Vincentz Gula. During a trip to Germany, Judy visited a medieval castle and saw this beautiful statue of Joan of Arc. After a little photo editing and manipulation, she printed the image on organza and layered the sheer fabric over painted fabric. The silk fabric and metallic embellishments echo the metals in the castle. *Courtesy of the artist.*

Nantucket by Jill Sheehan. This quilt is Jill's response to her local guild's quilt challenge on landmarks. The quilt depicts her sister-in-law's house in Nantucket where apparently by law all houses must be sided with unpainted cedar shingles — which weather to gray — and white trim. *Courtesy of the artist.*

I Find Refuge in Symbol by Catherine Kane. While on an Alaskan ferry, Catherine met artist Roderick Smith who was journaling and sketching the scenery. They discussed art and process; the title of this piece comes from Smith's journal with his permission. Kane often works from photographs. *Courtesy of the artist.*

Summerside II: Remembering our Beach Days by Mary Ellen Hardin Simmons. Mary Ellen visits Duck, North Carolina, with her family. On this trip in 2009, the group included seven grandchildren. In this quilt, Mary Ellen captured the feel of the rough water and her granddaughter's fearlessness. *Courtesy of the artist.*

Adirondack Black and Tan by Meghan J. Welch, quilted by Jean Welch. Quilters sometimes travel to retreats and camps to sew and enjoy creative friends. Meghan created this quilt, based on the "Habitat" pattern by Fourth and Six Designs, to remind her of the tranquil camp setting and constant encouragement of these yearly retreats in the Adirondack Forest. This calm and restful quilt is the second in her ongoing series of "quilt camp" quilts. *Courtesy of the artist.*

Some Celebration Quilts are designed to capture a moment in time. We revisit the happy events and use the quiltmaking process to help us heal from the tragedies. Both types of quilts are important.

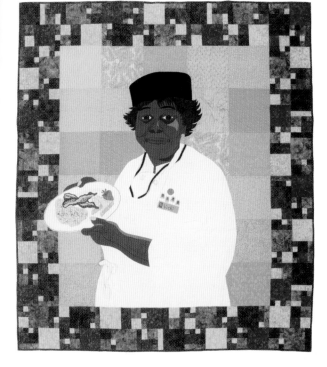

Miss Vicki by Shannon Shirley. For the six years preceding this quilt's creation, Shannon was greeted by Miss Vicki's cheerful smile over the breakfast buffet at the Mid-Atlantic Quilt Festival's host hotel. Every morning, Miss Vicki started the quilters' day with a happy greeting. To quote the artist, the Mid-Atlantic Quilt Festival wouldn't be the same without her! *Courtesy of the artist.*

Picking Up the Pieces: Tragedy and *Picking Up the Pieces: Recovery*, both by Cyndi Souder. Many of the quilters I know made quilts in response to the events on September 11, 2001. I couldn't decide if I needed to commemorate the tragedy of that day or pay tribute to the response of the American people. As a result, this quilt is double-sided. I used the black netting to symbolize smoke and other factors that obscured our vision.

Tsunami by Meghan J. Welch. Meghan created this quilt in response to the 2011 Tsunami in Japan, as well as an Art Quilt Study Group homework assignment to portray running or flowing water. She used her memories of the 2004 tsunami that struck Southeast Asia. At that time, she was a Naval Officer serving in a group sent to provide humanitarian aid and assistance to the hardest struck area of Indonesia. This quilt depicts the scene that confronted her there as well as the hope for aid and support from the world community. *Courtesy of the artist.*

Epilogue

With this Ring by Cyndi Souder.
Courtesy of Andrew Gay and Amy Rigney-Gay.

I find a special satisfaction in making Celebration Quilts. I know that when I present a Celebration Quilt, part of me goes with it, even if the quilt is going to a client. I try to make quilts the recipients would want to have as well as quilts I'm proud to make and present. It's especially rewarding to hear from the quilt's new owners after they've had their quilt for a while.

Both wedding quilts I made hang in the couples' homes. In one house, the quilt hangs in the entry hall; in the other house, the quilt hangs over the bedroom fireplace. I think it's risky to give an art quilt as a gift, but these two quilts were well received. They are seen and appreciated on a daily basis.

I asked people who have my baby quilts to send them back so that I could photograph them for this book. When they started to arrive at my home, I realized how long ago I had made some of them and how well-loved they are. The older ones are fading from the laundry, which makes me smile since I know they are being used. In some cases, the parents asked if I could hurry to return the quilts so that they would not be missed for too long.

My clients continue to say positive things about the quilts I've made them to honor their lost loved ones. One out-of-town client drove her quilt to the photo shoot so she would not have to risk shipping it. Another client still shares her quilt with first-time visitors to her home. I like to think their quilts helped them grieve and reminded them of the good times.

Teal Beauty continues to spark conversations. I share the story during some of my lectures, and I wonder how many of the quilters who expressed interest have gone on to participate in similar projects. Every once in a while, someone will ask when I'm going to make another quilt like *Teal Beauty*. The question is usually followed by an offer to help.

Celebration Quilts benefit the quilter as well as the recipient. They give form to our urge to help others, and they offer joy and comfort to those who need it. I hope you've enjoyed reading about the thought and creative process behind my work — and I hope you will use some of this information as you make your own Celebration Quilts.

Celebrate with quilts!

Resources

Blocks and Patterns:

• 501 ROTARY-CUT QUILT BLOCKS by Judy Hopkins will give you a treasure trove of traditional blocks with drawings, sizes, and re-sizing information.

• The pattern for so many of the star baby quilts I've made is "Lucky Stars" by Diane Atkinson at www.AtkinsonDesigns.com.

• For simple but effective quilt designs that will highlight special fabric collections or work well showcasing artifacts, check out the patterns by www.BlueUndergroundStudios.com.

• For more information on quilting basics, check out Pat Sloan's *I Can't Believe I'm Quilting: Beginner's Complete Guide*.

Favorite Online Sellers:

• For all things art quilt related, visit www.ArtisticArtifacts.com. Judy Gula, the proprietor, is my cofounder for Power Suits: An Art Quilt Challenge.

• The lovely Tiki roll I used in the *Strippy Baby Quilt* and some of the fabric for *Teal Beauty* came from www.SewBatik.com.

Quilt Projects and Collections:

• Learn more about Power Suits: An Art Quilt Challenge at www.PowerSuitQuilts.com.

• Learn more about Healing Quilts in Medicine at www.HealingQuiltsinMedicine.org.

Quilt to benefit others:

• The Alzheimer Art Quilt Initiative (www.alzquilts.org) collects priority quilts to raise awareness and fund research.

• Project Linus collects quilts for children who are seriously ill, traumatized, or otherwise in need. Visit www.ProjectLinus.org for more information.

• The mission of the Quilts of Valor Foundation is to cover all combat service members and veterans touched by war with comforting and healing Quilts of Valor. Visit www.qovf.org for more information.

Quilt to benefit others in your community:

• Local chapters of Habitat for Humanity work with local quilt guilds to provide quilts to families and children in their program. Details vary; contact your local chapter for more information.

• Some hospitals welcome donated quilts for their children's wards, NICU, and infusion centers. Contact hospitals directly for specific guidelines.

• Women's Shelters and Senior Citizens' Homes also welcome donated quilts. Contact your local organizations directly for more information.

Other Resources:

• For more information about the World Championship Punkin Chunkin, visit www.PunkinChunkin.com.

• To learn more about the Institute for Cancer Research or for information on how you can support them, visit www.icr.ac.uk.